The Rise and Fail of Charities
and What You Can Do to Be Ready

THE RISE AND FAIL OF CHARITIES

& What You Can Do To Be Ready

Wayne Elsey

WEE Publishing

ORLANDO

Published by WEE Publishing

520 N. Semoran Blvd., Suite 200, Orlando, FL 32807

ISBN: 978-0-578-16754-1

Dedication

In memory of my dad, who was my first role model.
He exemplified "being Christ like."
And to Bernard DeLoach, a family man,
visionary, loyal friend and thinker.

TABLE OF CONTENTS

Foreword

I first met Wayne Elsey at the American Airlines Admirals Club in Miami International Airport. Within five minutes, he was giving me grief and I simply didn't know how to take the guy. Here was a wildly successful philanthropic entrepreneur, someone by whom I should be intimidated, not giving me the opportunity to be intimidated. He had figured me out in the first thirty seconds of our meeting. I was impressed, and slightly irritated that I couldn't flash my mad defensive skills.

We were heading to Haiti, a place that became dear to the Soles4Souls founder's heart. The devastation from the 2010 Port-Au-Prince earthquake seemed to personally affect him greatly, and he threw his substantial philanthropic capital behind helping the Haitian people return to some semblance of normalcy. Wayne wanted to show the world the spirit of these battered but not broken souls, and I was there to film it.

Our flight down still didn't give me a good read on the guy. He was jovial, a prankster, almost silly. 'I hope he knows what he's doing,' I thought, wondering if he treated anything seriously. I would soon learn the truth: he knew exactly what he was doing at all times.

Arriving at a foreign airport can sometimes be a dicey proposition. Protocols are different, attitudes are different; I was afraid of doing the wrong thing or saying the wrong phrase. Within ten minutes of arriving, over fifty people from all walks of life had greeted him. "Wayne!" they shouted, followed by bear hugs all around. I was in good hands, and my worry abated.

Yet before I even had the chance to fully comprehend what was going on, we were beyond the pandemonium of the customs hall and entering into what would be one of the most unforgettable experiences of my life. It also reignited the fire to make the world a better place.

There were almost no words that could quite capture Haiti at that time; it was everything and nothing I thought it would be. Many parts were unsanitary beyond reason, with mounds of garbage larger than most cars on the side of the road or in vacant lots. There was gray water all around the city with no rain in sight. Many people still lived in makeshift huts made of plastic tarps, plywood and corrugated metal sheets. The most unforgettable punch in the gut was the smell; I learned to constantly breathe through my mouth for fear of falling down.

Once the shock-value of these new stimuli lifted, I saw the Haiti that Wayne saw: a country of people who still smiled when there was almost nothing earthly to smile about; a country of people who worked very hard for very little; a country of people who still believed in a better tomorrow; a country of people grateful for what little they had; a country of people grateful to people like Wayne who saw a need, and got off the couch to do something about that need.

That is actually what Wayne and I had most in common: to take a bad situation and turn it upside down. In 2002, I was diagnosed with Stage 3 Testicular Cancer. After a six-month battle to beat it, I was left with so many questions and no answers. In my quest to find those answers, I learned that a great many patients and survivors had my same experience, and they had no answers, either.

To change this, a television and film producer friend and I had a crazy idea to tell the story of my battle, to share with others my mistakes and pitfalls so that they might have the foresight to avoid the traps I not only fell into, but sometimes welcomed. A screenplay became a gateway for an idea to not only share stories, but to pay it forward with the profits of potential endeavors. The American Cancer Society and the IRS bought into what we were attempting, and before we knew it, we had achieved our own not-for-profit status.

Which is why, at times, it felt odd that I was helping Wayne with a mission that had absolutely nothing to do with our own mission. After interviewing him in the middle of the marketplace, I turned my camera off and asked him, "Wayne, do you think it's odd that we, who have a tiny little philanthropic mission, are helping you with your wildly successful philanthropic mission? Aren't we competing in a way?"

His answer floored me: "Dan, you're not my competition. Even other shoe organizations are not my competition. Right now, there are 287 million children without a single pair of shoes. My only competition is time."

And that is what has made my own journey with Wayne so unique. His outlook on philanthropy is a paradigm shift of everything we have been taught about the not-for-profit world: the sympathy to alleviate suffering, and the empathy to suffer along the way.

It is one thing to be a "do-gooder," which I don't see as a negative at all; the world needs more of us. However, if our quest to do well is hampered by our inability to grow our mission to not only sustainable, but also regenerating levels, then what good are we actually doing?

Once, we had the amazing fortune to meet an exceptionally successful Oscar winning producer from Hollywood. He had tried to get not-for-profit status for a film project, but the legal hoops his team would have to jump through made him "run out of my lawyer's office with my hair on fire, saying 'impossible.'"

I asked, "Was your film the absolute final goal?"

"It was," he said.

And there was his problem: his film was the end of the journey, not the end of the beginning of the journey. And that's really what our lives as philanthropists are: journeys. There are peaks and valleys and plains. There are the peaks when you get the attention of those who can really make things happen for you, and then there are the valleys of discovering that you have no idea how to leverage that attention.

And often, there are times when many, if not all of us, ask the hardest questions of all: "Are we making a difference? And if not, why are we even doing this?"

That is just one of the many things that Wayne has taught me on my own journey. I'm constantly learning new things, new strategies, and new ways to think about our mission and how to implement it for the long haul. His guidance and counseling has been invaluable. We would probably not exist today without him, and our goal is to, indeed, exist in a big way.

We want our mission to survive as long as there is a need, or they find a cure for cancer…whichever comes first. Because deep down, for us, it would be nice to eventually be irrelevant.

Dan Duffy, Co-Founder, The Half Fund

INTRODUCTION

Globally, the new century and millennium has ushered in enormous change in almost every facet of our existence. The nature of how we communicate, work, obtain information and learn has profoundly shifted.

As you read this book, you will see that I embrace change, welcome innovation, and believe in solutions. I am not a "Band-Aid" type of guy. There are many nonprofits out there that see someone hurting and provide a bandage to help ease the pain.

I would say to them, "God bless you. There's a place for you and a need for you."

However, this book is intended more for those who are looking to provide a cure, in addition to the Band-Aid. This book will challenge you to think big and go for it. I passionately believe that "nonprofit" is another word for "business." The most efficient, well-led, visionary "businesses" will make the biggest difference in this world. I also believe a few "great" nonprofits can reach millions and, in some instances, this is better than many small nonprofits who can reach a few.

Why?

Larger nonprofits may obtain and leverage greater resources.

With these larger organizations, we can seek the cures to what ails society. Still, there is room for the smaller "mom and pop" operations because often they are an important stitch in the fabric of a local community. Every neighborhood and town needs a small charity.

However, there is one key ingredient that both large and small organizations need, and that is vision. Nonprofits of any size require a range of view that aspires to do the simple, such as provide a Band-Aid, to the very great-improving a life.

You will also read that I talk a lot about today's donor, or "funder," who is looking for ways to solve problems—more than simply meeting an immediate need. This is because there is a very real discussion happening in the nonprofit sector about addressing the core issues that result in the symptoms.

Many funders today, particularly those who give substantial amounts of money, think in terms of "investment" and "return on investment" rather than in "meals served." In saying this, I recognize that there are still many donors, who may provide smaller dollar value gifts, which are no less significant. They want to respond and give to an immediate need.

These donors want to feed the hungry and clothe the naked, but I believe the future (and present) for nonprofits that want to grow and solve today's challenges rests in the giving profile of the "donor-funder," and not only in the "donor-responder."

For decades, the nonprofit sector focused on charity. Donors responded to this or that need. This is changing. Funders want to see systemic change. They are moving away from only addressing the symptoms. These types of donors are looking to help resolve the root cause of issues such as poverty, education, inequality and the environment.

The nonprofit sector is in the process of experiencing a paradigm shift. Donors who provide significant gifts in the five, six and seven-figure range are demanding more from organizations. In exchange, these types of donors want to see a "return." In other words, they want to know how a charity is measurably making a difference. They want results to be quantified. While the anecdote is important, they are looking more at the bottom-line numbers.

This paradigm shift is infusing itself slowly into the thinking of donors who may donate a couple of dollars or, perhaps several hundred. You will see as you read the book examples of smaller gift donors, or who are called in the business "general donors," who are not responding to the typical nonprofit approach.

There are many reasons for the changes that are afoot. Technology and innovation play an important part in this evolution. However, we are also dealing with a world that is increasingly connected, and this is bringing new voices with different world views to the forefront. So, what may have worked in the

The Rise and Fail of Charities and What You Can Do To Be Ready
Wayne Elsey

past for donors who tended to be of similar backgrounds is starting to evolve. Now, you have donors with varying perspectives and experiences who want to engage with your organization–large or small.

We live in exciting times and I firmly believe that we have the resources today to eradicate some diseases, provide work opportunities to working-age adults and help save the environment. We have the resources, today, to change the course of world history. But it takes big vision and commitment.

ONE
Loss of the Trust Capitol

Individual Donor: I donated to a charity the other day online and up pops up a window after I made the donation that they will be sending me a receipt in the mail. Why? It's wasteful and I would much rather have received an email acknowledgment.

Charlie's New Job

Recently I had a colleague named Charlie reach out to me. Charlie works in the nonprofit sector and fewer than six months ago he started a job working in a large charitable organization. Before working at the charity, he had been an independent consultant working with nonprofits and before that, he worked for a leading corporate-sponsored foundation.

It hasn't been easy for him to make the adjustment to his new environment, and he came to me looking for some advice on how to handle working for an organization that seems to be somehow stuck in the past.

"How's it going, Charlie," I asked.

"Could definitely be better," he replied pushing around the fork on his plate at the restaurant where we had lunch.

He looked like a beaten man.

Charlie spoke to me about proposals that he was drafting and how he was trying to change some of the language, which was dense and too academic. He has excellent experience in this because he worked in corporate funding. Charlie told me that in his experience, especially since he actually was on the other side of the table, corporations were looking for dynamic requests. They wanted easy to digest information.

We went back and forth on this and spoke about how corporations want to also associate themselves with organizations that help them look good.

"My boss is from the Stone Ages," he complained, "He's adamant about keeping this ridiculous language that is not serving them at all." The excuse was there really was no time for the organization to go through a vetting process on new language for proposals.

Charlie and I agreed this was a major mistake. And, I know it hurt Charlie to have the corporate funder experience and have his boss ignore that important background.

"Perhaps foundations are still willing to accept these sorts of proposals," he said, "But corporations are not looking for material they will have to read through only after three strong cups of coffee. Come on!" His frustration was evident.

He told me he thought this would actually begin to negatively impact the organization's bottom line. As a matter of fact, this was something that he was already starting to see when he analyzed the paucity of funding the organization had received from corporations.

I work with nonprofits every single day and I have seen this all too often. I understood what Charlie was telling me and although we came up with some strategies for him to use, no one knows what will ultimately happen. In other words, time will tell if Charlie's organization will see that doing things the way they have always been done is not an effective strategy in today's world.

I have a lot of experience in the corporate, nonprofit and social enterprise sectors and I know that funders want to trust that you are able to keep up with the times. Funders want to know that a nonprofit knows how to approach them!

Loss Of Trust

Around the time I connected with Charlie, I happened to hear an interview with Richard Solomons, Chief Executive Officer, InterContinental Hotels Group (IHG).

Essentially, what Mr. Solomons was speaking about was the fact that there has been an erosion of public trust across private and public institutions. I could not agree more. And, I would also say that this lack of trust, and all it represents, is significantly affecting the nonprofit sector. Charlie's story is just one of many. Innumerable nonprofits are still operating with "old school" thinking, practices and technology.

Last year Larry Page, the Founder and CEO of Google led a TED discussion, which are global conferences run by the nonprofit Sapling Foundation to help promote ideas throughout the world about a myriad of topics. Larry Page told attendees that he would rather give his fortune at the time of his death to a company rather than a nonprofit. Along with other global business leaders, he believes in "philanthrocapitalism." That's simply a fancy way of saying that philanthropy should be infused with some of the same principles, benchmarks and metrics that the for-profit world uses.

Why are all of these discussions happening?

Simple. There is a loss of trust that nonprofits can do the job.

Nonprofit fundraisers usually look at donors in two categories: major donors and general donors. Sure, there may be other segments, which nuance these two sets of donors more. Essentially, major donors donate at a high level (usually starting at $1,000 or $5,000 depending on the size of the organization. Then, there are general donors who tend to make up the bulk of donors to charity. These are the folks who donate less than these amounts to an organization. They may donate $10, $100 or $500.

There is a subtle shift occurring, and it is beginning with the major donors and is slowly permeating to the broader masses. These almost imperceptible changes are having a big impact because many of today's donors are looking to get to the root cause of societal challenges. While countless donors, particularly general donors, want to help meet the immediate needs of a charity there are others who want to go deeper into the issue.

So, for example, let's take education. You have major donors who are interested in systemic changes in education and they discuss school choice, the role of poverty in education, the role of teachers and parental involvement, etc. They are looking not only to address daily school performance, but the issues that impact a child's education particularly in a community with limited resources. In contrast, you have the vast majority of general donors who give to schools so children have meals after school and kids do not go to bed hungry, or they help teachers purchase school supplies.

This distinction is important so that as you read through this book, you understand my point of view. When I speak generically about "donors" or "funders," I am referring to the good portion of major donors and, more and more, the general gift donors who are looking for systemic change.

Increasingly, today's donors and philanthropists believe, as do I, that *non-*

profits are a business. Donors today want to talk about "investment," not charity. Honestly, if you look around, who wants to give because some nonprofit is holding out its old tin cup and asking, probably shyly, for charity? Charity is important, yes, but many people are now looking to go beyond the immediate need.

In the United States, and even much more graphically overseas, the public is subjected to images of dying children or abused animals. Organizations are asking for help–right now! I have a friend who says that when she sees these advertisements on the television, she switches the channel on the remote. She hates this type of plea. And, here's the thing. She never gives.

I asked her why.

"It's simple. They're giving me the old guilt trip to give to the child, but they never tell me what they're doing to solve the problem. They tell me a story of death, but they don't tell me a story of hope," she said. Who gives to death? People want to give to hope.

Does the "death" approach instill confidence in you that any given organization will actually alleviate whatever issue it is they seek to address? If you happen to give, more often than not, it's just a one shot deal. What about the hope of a better future for that child?

Increasingly, donors today believe in building a strong *philanthropic* infrastructure, as is done in business, so as to address the challenges of poverty, education, disease, etc. in a way that can be replicated and affect many people–not just a few.

Donors don't want to give yet another donation to save a child if tomorrow that same child will still be hungry. They want to support organizations that are looking to cure poverty, or greatly improve education!

Additionally, in many cases, providing services to 100 or 500 individuals each year is not enough. We need more organizations to be able to grow and expand their reach and impact because they are able to obtain greater resources that lead to systemic change.

Donors today know that nonprofits are not the only game in town. They believe in supporting *any* organization, including for-profit social enterprises that are able to make the largest impact. This means that for the investment they make, they are looking for an organization to be able to show high social "returns" and value, which is the nonprofit sector's version of "profits."

Funders today, including the foundation lead by EBay's founder, Pierre Omidyar, are prepared to invest their money into whatever organization they *trust* will be able to give them the results they want to see. They don't believe

The Rise and Fail of Charities and What You Can Do To Be Ready
Wayne Elsey

they are tied any longer to having to give to nonprofit's, especially if these nonprofits can't demonstrate they are willing and able to evolve with the times. These funders are providing directives to their staff to invest in whatever organization (for-profit or nonprofit) is able to demonstrate substantial results.

They want an end to poverty. They want an end to disease. They want an end to educational inequality. Increasingly, major and some general donors understand the importance of philanthropy. Yes, again, charity is important and addressing the immediate need, but so is the root cause of an issue.

Larry Page takes this distrust of nonprofits a step further. His view is that nonprofits have essentially lost their credibility to make changes on a global scale. In his view, businesses are also philanthropies if they are doing anything to better human kind and they have the ability to measure results and outcomes.

Before you tie yourself up in knots, if you are a nonprofit executive, and reach out to me to complain, I don't necessarily hold Mr. Page's view that corporations and businesses are also philanthropies. My main reason for this is simply because corporations are accountable to their shareholders and their highest purpose is to make money. However, for-profits may certainly have philanthropic intentions.

In my view, space can exist for both nonprofits and for-profit social ventures. We can have both nonprofit organizations, which exist solely to fulfill a social mission and for-profits that believe in wanting to change the world, empower people and make a profit.

Philanthropy

I think it's important to remind readers that there is a difference between "charity" and "philanthropy."

The word "philanthropy" has its origins in the Greek language and is credited to the Greek playwright Aeschylus who wrote "Prometheus Bound." Philanthropy simply means, "love of humanity" as it pertains to the caring and development of all humans. Philanthropy includes those who are in need and also those who give of their time or resources.

Charity is not necessarily philanthropic, although in the modern world the two have been conflated. Charity is narrower and seeks to address immediate pain and suffering. ***Philanthropy seeks to solve the issues at the root of the problem***. I think this is a really important distinction to make because I believe in philanthropy and some charity.

If you have read my previous book, *Almost Isn't Good Enough*, or visited my company websites or read some of my articles on by blog *Not Your Father's Charity*, you know that I believe very much in the spirit of teaching a man to fish rather than simply giving him a fish. I believe when there is a need to alleviate in charity, but the greater spirit of my thinking is to focus on philanthropy.

With that understanding, I do believe that companies can be philanthropic and socially minded. I also believe that nonprofits have provided an opportunity for social entrepreneurs and others to challenge the old nonprofit ways of doing things.

And, that is why you can have Larry Page thinking that he will not leave much, if anything, to charitable organizations. That's why he says he will seek to support visionary business leaders with a ***philanthropic*** interest.

More and more social enterprises are being established by leading professionals who are socially aware and seek to make a global impact.

Again, why has all of this happened? Because there is a lack of public trust, and in this case, there is lack of trust in what nonprofits can accomplish.

Sure, both public and private organizations have lost public trust. I'm not saying that for-profit companies and social enterprises are perfect. But, companies have the investment capital, ingenuity and flexibility to try to do better. In the meantime, many nonprofit leaders continue to do business as they have always done it and don't see the tsunami that is coming to their shores.

The Changing World

One of the thought leaders sounding the alarm in the nonprofit sector is activist Dan Pallotta, Founder, Charity Defense Council. His organization seeks to treat nonprofits as businesses and wants donors to make significant investments in them. Dan, along with other leaders in the nonprofit sector want to end the cycle that rewards organizations for how little they spend as opposed to the impact they make.

While my friend, Dan, calls out donors who are concerned with making sure nonprofits spend the vast majority of money on direct program related expenses; I also think that nonprofit professionals themselves share the blame in this situation.

Generally speaking, nonprofits have failed to consistently explain and educate donors and the public as to why they require money for "overhead." They have failed to explain why it is important to invest in a nonprofit business. They have not educated donors enough so they understand they need to hire the best people, scale up their organizations and continually seek to research and develop more effective ways to accomplish their goals.

This didn't just happen to the nonprofit sector. It didn't happen *to* them. They let it happen, and they are paying the consequences.

Each day, I work with nonprofits. I speak to nonprofit executives; learn about current trends and am continually immersed in ways to do things better for people around the world in order to empower them. But, sometimes, as I reflect on a given week, I am disappointed to see that many nonprofits remain in the "polyester days." As the world moves forward at warp speed, many nonprofit executives are inadvertently helping global leaders and philanthropists like Larry Page, and others, question their very existence.

Trust capital is lacking.

Let's go back in time.

Just ten years ago, you listened to your music on CDs. If you were really ahead of the curve, you had recently purchased an iPod Mini. You may have carried a mobile flip phone or a heavy personal device assistant (PDA). You took pictures using a digital camera.

Mark Zuckerberg's "the facebook" was in its early stages. In August of 2005 it became Facebook.

Business professionals carried around pagers and bulky Blackberry mobile phones, with Motorola Moto Razr V3 and its sleek design creating a cult fan base. Smartphones had been in existence since the early 1990's, but they were in their infancy. Steve Jobs and the engineers at Apple were still a number of years out from revolutionizing the field with the iPhone.

We had not yet lived through the Great Recession and the incredible disruption and innovation that were created as a response to the changing times. People still looked at their careers before 2008 as ones where they would have only few career changes. They had no idea about how they would soon have to become their own personal brand and employment consultant with multiple career changes.

What about the nonprofit and international NGOs?

In 2005, we were only a handful of years into a new century and millennium. The nonprofit sector was very much doing things with 20th Century thinking and technology.

Proposals were submitted on paper and collateral material was given to people in their hands. Direct mail was the most important part of the overall fundraising revenue equation. Many organizations were choosing to do the majority of their communication with their donors and constituents through postal mail.

By the turn of this century, the nonprofit field was continuing to become more professionalized. Professionals with college and graduate degrees in the social sciences were leading organizations. A few executive directors and CEOs were starting in increasing numbers to obtain graduate degrees in business.

What do I see today?

Unfortunately, I still see many nonprofit organizations that don't understand or invest in technology. Don't bring me paper, which needlessly kills trees. If I am meeting with you and you want me to get involved with you, show me what you are talking about with your mobile or tablet device.

I see executive directors who are fearful of asking for investment money. They still have a "tin cup" mentality and are not comfortable with investment. They feel very uncomfortable about having to ask for money and they fail to articulate for donors (investors) why they need more from them.

Many nonprofits cannot see beyond their block. They may ease someone's curiosity and claim how involved they are in social media, but they don't realize that social media is global. So, when I ask them how they are reaching out to followers from all around the world, they reply that they focus on those who reside in their city. Have they not seen that a tweet they put out in the afternoon in an American city can be re-tweeted by someone in early morning on the other side of the world?

I see tension between Baby Boomers and Millennials. Nonprofits, being conservative by nature, don't want to rock the boat. But, they are not fostering an environment, which brings together the best attributes of the Boomers with those of the 20-something generation who have a vastly different world-view. And, of course, not much is ever said about the people who are now taking up leadership positions in society, Generation X.

As social enterprises and corporate social responsibility programs grow within the for-profit sector, many nonprofits are barely paying attention. This is not going away.

California, for example, is a state that has changed its laws to accommodate the existence of social enterprises. Other states have done the same. In other words, governments are increasingly changing laws to accommodate hybrid entities that are not wholly for-profit or nonprofit. Nonprofits are not the only kid on the block anymore.

Many nonprofits are charities, but they are not philanthropies. I speak to them every single day and so many nonprofit staff members are looking to only alleviate today's problem, but they are not looking at the root cause of the situation. We need charities, but we must push for a greater philanthropic vision in order to truly change the world.

Not too long ago, I was talking to a friend about charities and philanthropies. She is a veteran fundraiser and she said, "Wayne, you're spot on. A study from Compass found that 41 percent of nonprofits did not have a 'culture of philanthropy.'"[1]

That is a significant failure and challenge, in my opinion, for nonprofits.

How can anyone trust in the ability of many nonprofits to make a global difference when they're still going to work in polyester suits doing the same old thing? How can you trust an organization that claims to be looking at the bigger picture, but is not really looking to address the cause of an issue?

In the minds of the general public, the media, government, donors, business leaders and supporters, nonprofits that are failing to operate within the new paradigm of the 21st Century poison the well for the sector as a whole. In other words, one bad apple tends to ruin the whole bunch. People start to think there are better ways to do things and the conversation begins to be held with many nonprofits left out of the dialogue.

In order for the sector as a whole to advance in the hyper-competitive and global world that exists today, they need to work on developing and increasing their trust capital.

---

1   "Underdeveloped: A National Study of Challenges Facing Nonprofit Fundraising," Compass Point and Evelyn and Walter Haas, Jr. Fund, 2013, http://www.compasspoint.org/sites/default/files/images/UnderDeveloped_CompassPoint_HaasJrFund_January%202013.pdf

TWO
The "F" Word

Nonprofit Staff Member: I just got out of school and I was excited when I started with my current organization. Now, I'm looking for another job. I don't get it. When I suggest an improvement, I kind of feel like I'm just the new kid that no one needs to listen to. I wouldn't want to get involved with them down the line when I make more money.

Playing It Safe

"F" is for failure.

Terrible word, isn't it? No, it's not. There is no success without failure and nonprofits have a way of running from failure. As an industry, organizations are risk averse and they would rather do anything but fail. Yes, failure does have consequences, but business is about failure, and nonprofits are a business.

When for-profit businesses fail, they don't simply take their marbles and go home or hide under a rock. They learn from past mistakes and they build upon the experience.

One of my favorite quotes about failure comes from Max Levchin, Pay-Pal co-founder: "The very first company I started failed with a big bang. The second one failed a little less, but still failed. The third one, you know, proper failed, but it was kind of okay. I recovered quickly. Number four, almost didn't fail. It still didn't feel great, but it did okay. Number five was PayPal."

Nonprofits hardly ever want to speak about failure. It's common knowledge that 80 percent of businesses will fail within their first five years. I believe it is at least that rate, if not more, in the nonprofit sector. A lot of it is simply because many nonprofits are stuck in the past with the same old mindset. This is fostering an environment where other types of entities such as social enterprises and corporations are stepping in to take the lead.

I'm not sure many nonprofits even realize that their fears and "play it safe" strategy are having unintended consequences. An environment now exists where donors and the public are starting to support other types of organizations. These donors seek more thought leadership, transparency and accountability and when they don't find it with nonprofits, they go elsewhere.

Again, there is a deficit of trust capital with regard to what nonprofits can truly accomplish in today's environment. Social enterprises and businesses are stepping in to take advantage of the opportunity created.

Midwest Nonprofit

Let me give you some concrete examples of major nonprofit organizations that have refused to acknowledge failure. By the way, this usually begins at the top with leadership.

For the sake of transparency for the reader, I will change some of the background about the nonprofits so they are not identifiable, but I will keep the failures accurate to make my point that many of today's nonprofits have not entered the 21st Century.

One organization in the Midwest is a nonprofit that was established nearly 40 years ago. The founder, who left only a handful of years ago, was a charismatic and passionate leader; however, the time had come for her to move on.

The board of this nonprofit underwent a national search to find the new chief executive. It was a sham, and if I were a donor or supporter, I would be pretty upset.

Since all of these board members had been with the organization for at least 10 years, the die was already cast. They wanted the man who had been serving as the organization's chief operating officer. They went about hiring a search firm and conducting a national search for the sake of appearances.

How would you like to be a donor to this organization and learn that money was spent needlessly for this phony search? They had made the decision before the recruitment process even began to select the COO.

Within a few months, predictably, the organization promoted the chief operating officer. During his three-year tenure, he has so far managed to oversee an agency that went from a $30 million operating budget to one of $20 million.

The entire senior management staff, and much of the junior team, has left the organization, usually under contentious circumstances. With them, an incredible amount of institutional knowledge has disappeared. These staff separations have also been antagonistic and word is out on the street about the internal mess.

Board meetings have become utterly dysfunctional. Factions have developed seeking to blame anyone but the board–or the current CEO–for the spectacle that has been created.

Staff walk into board meetings with the clear understanding that it could very well be the defining moment and demise of their own position within the organization. They talk about wearing "bullet proof vests." Huh? This is a nonprofit, not some place with guerrilla warfare.

The board had worked with the new CEO for years in his capacity as COO. They absolutely knew exactly who he was and they were also well aware that he was and always should be, an administrator. He never demonstrated any management or leadership talent.

He was great at being the second in command. However, they did not want someone coming in from the outside with new ideas who would, inevitably, change things. They wanted to retain the status quo at all costs.

The former COO does not have the personality traits to make him a leader. One or two brave board members who opposed his selection voiced this concern, only to be sidelined.

The new CEO started out saying the right things, but his actions have been devastating to the organization. He spoke about diversifying income and the responsibility of leaders to change and innovate. Yet, nearly every incumbent or new professional hired or retained to help lead the change has been fired or let go.

The insistence that processes and procedures continue that were done in the 1980's and 1990's (that's not a typo) is mind-blowing. It is simply because the current CEO does not have a grasp or understanding of today's best business practices, technology and the world in which he lives. Since he does not comprehend it, he will stick with what he knows as the organization loses incredible amounts of traction, trust capital and ground to competitors.

The board refuses to accept their role or responsibility in this failure and fiasco. Their insistence on staying with someone they knew despite his deficits for the sake of their own comfort borders on reckless at best. Essentially agreeing with the new CEO not to change with the times and not seeking to be innovative and fresh is killing the organization by a thousand cuts.

This is an extreme, but actual, example of a nonprofit that is so entrenched in the polyester days that my prediction is within the next year or two it will have to close its doors. It has failed to go with the times, and there are other organizations, including social enterprises that can fill their space and deliver their services more efficiently.

Disappearance Of The Founder

At another nonprofit, the founder was someone who was innovative and forward thinking. In a handful of years, he was able to expand the organization from zero in revenue to $50 million. It was an incredible feat, considering the vast majority of nonprofit organizations never grow beyond the $1 million mark.

This CEO saw an opportunity and a need to be filled. He was able to use his past experience and knowledge from the for-profit sector and bring it to the nonprofit arena. The founder worked tirelessly and recruited the top people in the field. He believed in making an "investment" and when he asked for money, he talked about investment in infrastructure, scalability (growth), results and impact.

He tried new things, failed, communicated and implemented lessons he learned and built upon the experiences. Although he had some detractors, because there will always be naysayers when someone is succeeding, he was able to take a small entity and develop it into an international nonprofit juggernaut.

After several years, he decided to move on, partly because he knew he preferred and was better suited to building start-up organizations. There were new things to do on the horizon. As it happened, some on the board resigned once the founder exited the organization because there was a certain cult of personality with the charismatic former CEO.

Those who remained on the board decided to hire someone with extensive nonprofit experience. But, they failed to recruit a person who was innovative and as dynamic as the former CEO. Before leaving, the founding CEO provided the board new potential opportunities he was developing so they could continue to explore them and grow the organization.

The new opportunities, had they been taken in total, would have likely *doubled* the organization in size. Instead, the new CEO with the support of the board shut *all* of the new opportunity discussions down.

Want to know why?

They were not the new CEO's original ideas. This was an incredible failure of vision and the first signal to anyone who was paying attention that the current CEO was insecure.

The organization had been founded with visionary core principles of philanthropcapitalism, being global, growing to scale, using technology effectively, being innovative and flexible, demonstrating impact and results and being a thought leader in the space.

Today, the organization is actually losing money and as each year passes, it is being compounded. It exists, but it has not been able to expand, and in fact, it is contracting at an alarming rate.

Morale is at a low point. Staff has started to head for the doors and the CEO's continued lectures on visionary leadership are now viewed as comical in light of the lack of effective action.

Inconsistency rules the day. On the one hand, the current CEO has removed all mention of the founding CEO from the collateral material, including the website. But, most bizarrely, anything that goes wrong, even years after the founder left, are the supposed failing legacy of the former CEO. You can't have it both ways.

Many things that were originally in place by the former CEO have been dismantled and the new CEO has taken a much more traditional nonprofit stance on growth and fundraising. He speaks about donations, as opposed to investments. He looks to provide charity. The messages of empowerment and philanthropy are gone. People have seen this and they have stepped away.

Failures Are Okay

Where is the leadership?

Where is the acceptance of failure?

Failure is a part of the success process and it needn't be looked at as a dirty word.

In both cases, the reality of business and life itself is that people do get tired of lip service. Eventually, what you say does not matter, especially if it is not backed up with clear and intentional action.

In each, the board needs to reflect in the mirror and see that they too are responsible for the decreasing revenue, lack of momentum and energy that have hit their teams. In the two organizations, you have nonprofit leaders who are in the business of blaming others and not looking at their own performance. In these instances, failure is seen as a curse. Outdated and limited thinking has clearly brought about these failures.

But failure is also an opportunity. If you had true leaders at the helms of each organization to discard what is not working and look to grow and become truly sustainable beyond the dysfunction, you may be able to see success.

I understand why nonprofits don't want to fail. It hurts. And, for nonprofits, it can bring bad press and dilute or even place nonprofits in a precarious position with funding dollars. Donors don't really like it when money is lost on a program or initiative that did not work. However, savvy nonprofits partner with funders when they are looking to develop new efforts to pilot them first or work with funders on the evaluation.

Nonprofit organizations should try new things. They should develop new ways of doing things and seek to have more investment into their planning, research and development.

Be the first one on the block to develop a new way to address an old problem. If it works, funders will come running!

Organizations should transparently ask for investment money for the analysis of performance metrics and evaluation as well. And, trying new initiatives also means, nonprofits can learn from the mistakes and improve upon them.

Susan G. Komen Breast Cancer Foundation

Nancy G. Brinker established the Susan G. Komen Breast Cancer Foundation in 1982 with $200 and a list of donor prospects in memory of her sister, Susan, who had died of cancer in 1980. Nancy made a promise to her dying sister that she was going to do everything she could to eradicate cancer.

Since its establishment the organization, which was re-branded to Susan G. Komen for the Cure, over $2.5 billion has been invested into research, community outreach and advocacy around the world. This has not happened without failure and controversy.

In 2010, Susan G. Komen was considered one of the most trusted nonprofits in the United States. A handful of years later, it was dropped as one of the most trusted 4 star charities by Charity Navigator, a leading nonprofit information provider for donors, due to criticism about the use of funds.

Additional critiques about the organization include its sponsor affiliations and its cause marketing. In 2012, Susan Komen sought to withdraw funding from Planned Parenthood, only to run headlong into a withering firestorm, which prompted it to quickly change course.

Whether or not you agree with Susan G. Komen, they are out there making mistakes, but learning and moving forward. They have donors who are completely committed and supportive of their work and they continue to do the walks and runs.

Just this year, they created a partnership with Drexel University College of Medicine. If you see where they are today, after some missteps, they are still flooding the country with pink ribbons and their efforts to fulfill Nancy Brinker's promise to do everything in her power to eradicate cancer.

Nonprofit Fails

Clearly, nonprofits or initiatives fail for a variety of reasons. In my experience some of the main culprits, which stem from leadership, vision and innovation, are the following:

- Core mission or objectives – Sometimes success can exact a price, as does failure. Leaders can become distracted and focused on only resolving a problem or seeking to do substantially better than the previous year or project. This can cloud judgment. Nonprofit executives need to be vetting strategic decisions and positions related to course of action on an ongoing basis. They need to reach out to supporters and ask for opinions before the genie is out of the bottle.

- Skilled and qualified leadership – Probably the main reason in my estimation that nonprofits fail is because they have entrusted the organization to an executive who is simply not up to the task of leading. Typically, they do not lack the technical expertise to do the job, but they fail because they lack the ever-important leadership skills to motivate others to follow their lead. Another problem nonprofits have, is that nonprofits recruit board members who themselves are not qualified or understand this position of responsibility.

- Money – Many nonprofit organizations live in a perpetual state of crisis, and a lot of it has to do with money. Instead of having a healthy relationship with money, they create an environment where philanthropy is somehow lost in translation. Strategic focus and development of key areas of revenue are not concretely planned for and the conversation with financial supporters never moves from the tin cup mentality of charity. This happens in a world that is increasingly infusing capitalistic principles into a conversation about philanthropy as a whole.

- Awareness of the competition – In today's world, nonprofits need to understand that corporations, businesses and social enterprises are stepping into the game. These organizations are bringing new ways of approaching the same challenges as they relate to poverty, education, health, the arts or the environment. Nonprofits tend to focus on the day to day and they fail to see the opportunity for partnership with another entity that may be doing something better. They are also late in the game of seeing who might be doing better than them and, thus, is getting the majority of the donor market share. Always know your competition. You may be able to strike a partnership or see how they are addressing something and, perhaps, you can do it better.

• Donor-centricity – In the last 10 years, major donors have changed dramatically, and general donors are also beginning to shift what was once the "typical" donor profile. Nonprofits have to contend with the Millennials who are completely different with regard to how they want to be involved with organizations making an impact on society. Organizations also have to know how women and other "minority" groups, who are increasingly voicing their opinions and taking their rightful positions in the boardroom, want to support philanthropy. These groups have a different world view than the previous conventional donor. Add to that, a demand for more business oriented, transparent and accountability principles and many nonprofits are simply missing the boat on today's donors. Here's a hint, ***they are not all the same and you need to approach them differently***.

• Quantified Impact and Results – many nonprofits, as I have stated, do not quite understand the defining interest of today's donor, across all donor profiles and backgrounds. Donors today want to see measurable results and impact. Due to the trust capital that has been lost, they no longer take anyone's word at face value. They want results and they want proof of results. They want to know this as it relates to the impact of programs, but they also want to know this as it relates to a nonprofit's financials. They want to know that it costs $2 a day to give a child a chance at an education, for example, and they want to know the quantifiable impact of the child's education on the mission of the organization.

If you want your nonprofit to be competitive in today's environment and lead the way in the 21st Century, then you need to become comfortable with failure. There is simply no possibility for success without the courage to fail. Period.

The Rise and Fail of Charities and What You Can Do To Be Ready
Wayne Elsey

THREE
Passion and Trust Capital

Nonprofit Founder: I have been trying for 5 years to get this organization off the ground. I am lucky that I have a few donors who have been supporting the work. But, I just can't seem to figure out, or ever have enough money, to be able to get beyond helping just 50 kids.

I have been fortunate in my life. I learned very early by a happy accident that I would become a shoe salesman. I was 15 years old and I took a work-study opportunity that was available to me at the time. It was not long before I was essentially managing the store, although I could not hold the title because of my age.

I knew that selling shoes was what I wanted to do. Every day, women would come into my store and I would care about their needs and what they wanted. My customers saw that I cared about their best interest. When I spoke to them and asked them questions about the shoes, it was not simply, "How do they fit?"

They would walk in front of the mirror with their shoes and I would ask them, "Where do you see yourself wearing these shoes? Are they to go out for dinner, work or to have around the house?" It was more than a matter of how it made them **look**, but rather how did it make them *feel*.

They would tell me a narrative and I ultimately realized that as each customer and I talked about the shoes, each pair of shoes began to develop its own personal story for the wearer. My customers saw the passion and care I had for my work and they appreciated that I did not only see the functional side to shoes. They liked developing the story about how the shoes made them feel. This passion, told in a story, I believe is the foundation of what is necessary for trust capital.

The best stories about people, business and history itself involve stories that, at the core, translate the drive and determination–the passion–that someone has to do something or overcome a challenge. That is why we love stories of courage and honor.

People can spot a fake. On the other hand, people can easily see if you are interested or care in making your work better with vision and determined purpose. In today's world, pretenders can be quickly and publicly taken to task for better or worse.

Passion is the essential ingredient toward building trust. Why? Because even when times are tough, even when you fail, people are willing to work with you and forgive failings if they see that you really care. In addition, passion is what helps drive vision and the story you need to get people to support you. You can't get anywhere without it.

Do you see your organization wanting to serve 10 children, a classroom or a school? Do you see trying to address the immediate needs, or once those are being met, working to address the greater philanthropic needs of the people being served?

Recently, I came across an article about how cancer cases have increasingly grown at an alarming rate. There was a time when it was much more likely to be diagnosed with cancer if you had a genetic history of cancer in the family. While this is still accurate, there are ever more cases of people who have no family history of cancer receiving the dreaded diagnosis.

Game Changing

Cancer is a game-changer. I think it is fair to say that if you are reading this book, you probably know someone who has battled or died of cancer, or maybe you have been affected yourself.

I think most of us have had some sort of experience with the ravages of cancer. It is an insidious and devastating disease. Although I have been fortunate not to have personally fought cancer, I have walked this path with others who have died, are still battling the Big C or have kicked it to the curb, hopefully forever.

But there is something interesting that I have seen with cancer: clarity, purpose, passion to live or the courage to die on ones own terms. Wrapped in the enigma that is cancer, there are countless stories of passion and trust: passion to live a different way or to achieve the unthinkable. Trust in the process.

Although my businesses are not directly related to cancer awareness, prevention and research, people I have known with cancer have provided me with incredible inspiration and lessons about trust and passion for my personal life as well as my businesses. They are examples of the compelling stories nonprofits have to communicate in telling their own story and accomplishing their work. It's all about passion and drive. With that comes the human story and people trust in that vision.

Let me explain what I mean.

What I have learned is that there is nothing like cancer to put things quickly in perspective. The very mention of cancer just makes everything that you thought was important suddenly be not so important.

We all have this life and swirl that goes around us. We are busy with our families. We are busy with our businesses and work. We present this image to the world based on what we see for ourselves and, sometimes, on what others see for us. Transparency itself may become a relative term and in that, so does trust.

I think we can all agree that we are living in a new world where transparency is critically important. It is easy to do some quick research and see examples of how a business, government or individual were promptly brought to task for failing to be transparent about something that was deemed as important. Trust, which is a fragile thing, suddenly swept away in an instant.

Cancer has a way of doing that as well. It has a way of stripping away everything we thought about so-called reality and putting a focus on where things are truly important. It has a way of focusing us like a laser on what we truly care and are passionate about in our lives. This is a silver lining in the battle and I have seen my friends and colleagues focused on staying the course, living true to their personal mission and passions.

That is what nonprofits need to do.

Passion helps drive the story that people want to support. It helps build trust. Nonprofits need to change their perspective and thinking specific to their organization and the broader community around them. They need to rid themselves of the myopic disease that makes them afraid, muster the courage to fight hard and tackle it.

In order to start to make the necessary changes a nonprofit needs to survive in today's world, you first have to know there is a problem, and an opportunity. You have to become clear and recommitted not only to your mission, but also to your passion for that mission and doing everything possible to serve the broadest possible audience for your work.

That means working things differently. Being agile and flexible. And it means consistently pushing the envelope. Showing up to work with a polyester mind to deal with 21st Century challenges and opportunities is simply not going to cut it.

Dan Duffy And The Half Fund

Dan Duffy is a filmmaker and the founder of The Half Fund and a good friend of mine. The goal of this nonprofit is to "lift the veil on cancer" and provide opportunities for people to be able to support each other through this process by way of movies, books and music.

Dan and I are working together through my organization, Funds2Orgs. Dan had the benefit of traveling to Haiti in 2012 to film a documentary and it happens to be one of the countries where I work with micro-entrepreneurs.

Haiti is a country of less than 10 million people and one of the poorest nations in the Western Hemisphere. 72 percent of the population lives on fewer than $2 a day. Job opportunities are scarce in Haiti.

Funds2Orgs is an organization I established to support micro-enterprise in developing nations, the environment and nonprofits here in the United States and other developed nations, but I will write a little later in this book more about our work.

In 2012, Dan visited Haiti and learned about how shoes save lives. Around the world, 300 million children and their families are too impoverished to purchase a pair of shoes. If you are a parent, you know how quickly children grow. So not only is one purchase of shoes a challenge for the poorest among us, but there is also an ongoing need of shoes for growing feet.

But, this lack of safe, sturdy footwear has consequences. Walking shoeless risks parasitic diseases, which if left untreated may result in grave illness or even death. Without shoes, a child cannot attend school and individuals of working age cannot work.

After Dan visited Haiti, he immediately set out to work collecting shoes. He focused on his son's school and he was able to gather 700 pairs of shoes. But that wasn't enough. There's so much more to do! Today, he is working on collecting *1 million pairs of shoes* (40 tractor trailer loads), which will be shipped to the poorest developing nations.

Dan could have simply raised money for his organization, The Half Fund, the usual way. He was able to think out of the box and innovatively find a unique way to raise money for his nonprofit. By working with Funds2Orgs, he is also able to extend social good to Haiti, where he found a passion.

Fund2Orgs pays The Half Fund for all of the collected shoes by weight and Dan's nonprofit can continue its work of spreading awareness and providing support for those afflicted with cancer.

I know this may sound self-serving because I started Funds2Orgs. But, I am proud to partner with Dan and The Half Fund because he trusted us in providing him with an alternative to the same old event, email solicitation letter or telephone request asking for financial support. He decided to change the fundraising game with an audacious goal of collecting 1 million pairs of shoes and allowing donors to keep their wallets closed and instead use shoes as the currency for support.

In the meantime, Dan does his work in the development and distribution of his film about cancer, *Half*, which is a comedy film. It tells the story of a young man who wins his battle with testicular cancer. They are seeking to raise $750,000 for the film, at which point, they will make a donation to the American Cancer Society. Once the film is produced, released and distributed, they will make additional donations to that organization of all net profits.

Dan states on The Half Fund website, "I hated that cancer was so reactive. You never knew what nasty sneak-attack was going to come around the bend to jack you square in the face, and you didn't know what it was going to be, or how to fend it off. Most times, you didn't even know what hit you. There is no foresight when you're in the battle, and that's what bothered me the most."

And that is why I wanted to mention Dan in the course of this book. He eloquently explains the reactive nature of how things can be in life—and at work. In the case of nonprofits, many are constantly in crisis point and sometimes not sure of what to do next.

So many nonprofit organizations, as I have mentioned, are in a daily battle for survival, and it is a reactive instead of a proactive fight. I think this point is lost on many outside of the sector.

If you have the opportunity to speak to nonprofit executives each day, as I do, you will quickly learn that they are in "survival mode." Remember, the vast majority of nonprofits operate with revenues of less than $1 million. These organizations are feeling the heat of government funding cutbacks and lack of money. They are so busy fighting the pitched battle to survive that most of the time they don't have the ability to be thinking about the strategy.

Dan has had support and during those times when he was not able to know where the next punch was coming, he had others who were looking out for him. And that is an important point.

Nonprofit executives need to be able to open up and be clear about the battle they are waging, and they need to be clear about what it takes not only to survive, but also to make a measurable impact in the near and long term.

What Dan is doing with his film is he is taking a humorous look at a very painful disease and its effects. He is letting people know the reality. On the other hand, nonprofit executives in general, tend to not want to say what pains them or where they are failing–back to the "f" word.

This lack of transparency helps exacerbate the lack of trust capital. And because they are not being fully transparent and clear, they are finding themselves increasingly on the losing end of opportunity. More and more business-oriented non-profits and for-profits are entering the space to compete against them as it relates to making a significant and sustaining societal impact.

Like Dan, nonprofits need to be aggressive about explaining their vision, needs and deficits. They need to communicate on a much deeper and more meaningful level. If they don't, their supporters will simply turn to other organizations that are meeting their needs.

Teri Griege And The Ironman World Championship

Teri Griege is an inspiration and someone who puts it all out there. Her drive and passion are infectious. Teri is also a very good friend of mine who began running marathons in her forties, including the prestigious Boston, Chicago and New York races.

Based on Teri's own telling of her story, those events piqued her interest about triathlons and she committed herself to participate in the Ironman World Championship in Hawaii. In her preparation for that race, she worked on qualifying in the races leading up to the great race. She participated in the Ironman Louisville 2008 race only to miss qualifying for Hawaii by five minutes.

She was determined to get there, however, and over the course of the next year, she trained harder. During her punishing training regiment, she suffered minor injuries and setbacks, but kept going. However, she was more tired than usual, but thought it was simply a matter of "overtraining."

She was wrong.

After completing the 2009 Ironman in Louisville and clocking in ten minutes slower than the previous year despite the fact she had trained more and was better conditioned, she knew there was a problem. Something just was not right and she went to the doctor.

She was diagnosed with Stage 4 colon cancer, which had metastasized to her liver. She was given a 6 percent chance of survival and two years to live.

Like Dan and every courageous person I know who has received a diagnosis of cancer, she was not ready to give up without a fight. In addition, she was not going to give up on her dream, her passion or her story. She was given a special invitation to compete in the Ironman World Championship as an inspirational athlete. And, she accepted.

During the course of chemotherapy, radiation and colon and liver resections, she trained for this punishing race. And, instinctively knowing there was no way she could do this alone, she amassed an "army of supporters." They helped to motivate her, spot pitfalls and challenges that she may have missed and simply supported her in every way imaginable–even on those days when she felt she was failing.

And, on October 2, 2011, Teri completed the famed Ironman race in Kona, Hawaii. She was 50 years old.

Teri is beating cancer every day and, today, she continues with maintenance chemotherapy.

If you ever have the opportunity to meet Teri, you will meet someone who is humble. She herself says she is not superwoman. She is simply someone who decided, against all odds, to fight and do the unexpected. She was not willing to accept the inevitable and she knew she wanted to do more. Perhaps someone else would have received the same diagnosis as Teri and would have concentrated, rightly, on only trying to survive.

What I found remarkable is that no matter what, Teri kept her eye on the prize, the Kona Ironman race, and she would not be denied. She got supporters and told them of the good and the bad, the successes and failures and always the story of her passion.

Today, Teri travels the country speaking about the lessons she learned about overcoming obstacles, fear and doubt to do what many people would think of as impossible. She has been featured on media programs, including "The TODAY Show" on NBC.

Among the many things Teri says, there is one thing that I find to be a jewel, and that is from weakness comes perspective. Again, there is a great message.

Nonprofit organizations should be in the business of asking for support and assistance, even when their instincts are to show great success. They have to be willing to speak about their successes, their failures and their desires to go places they have never been in support of the work they do.

Like Teri and Dan, it is being able to tell your story–warts and all–with sincerity and passion to overcome that creates the foundation for getting other people on-board and involved. It is that infectious drive to succeed and clarity of vision, coupled with integrity, that builds the trust capital. Without those ingredients, everything is just an academic exercise.

Nonprofits can do this.

Make-A-Wish

Make-A-Wish is one of the largest charities in the United States. It all started in 1980. During a stakeout, U.S. Customs Agent, Tommy Austin, told Arizona Department of Public Safety Officer, Ron Cox, the story of Chris Greicius. At the time, young Chris was only seven years old and he was dying of cancer. Chris had a dream, however. He wanted to be a police officer "to catch the bad guys."

Tommy, whose wife was friends with Chris' mother, was trying to make the boy's dream come true, but he was having a very tough time getting through the bureaucracy and wondered if somehow Ron's law enforcement offices might be able to help.

And with that simple request made through the chain of command, a dying boy received his wish. Chris received a "Smokey Bear" hat, an old badge and to this day, Chris remains the only honorary Department of Public Safety officer in Arizona.

Chris also received a custom uniform that was worked on through the night due to his grave illness and on May 3, 1980 he died with his motorcycle officer wings and the experience of having become an honorary officer and being given so many gifts and mementos to commemorate this special wish.

That was only the beginning of the story for Make-A-Wish. So many officers and volunteers had been moved by what was done for Chris and they started to figure that these sorts of wishes could be given to other children.

In the United States, over 226,000 children threatened with life-threatening illness have received a wish. On average Make-A-Wish grants a wish every 38 minutes.

With clear drive for purpose, this organization has grown into a juggernaut with the establishment of Make-A-Wish International under which 48 affiliates throughout 5 continents in 48 countries operate. Collectively, around the world, Make-A-Wish has granted the wishes of over 310,000 children worldwide. Make-A-Wish America is one of the largest nonprofits in the country with revenue exceeding $265 million.

No one can tell me that this story cannot be replicated by visionary, passionate and determined nonprofits with other missions.

According to the *Stanford Social Innovation Review*[2], "Since 1970, 46,000 for-profits have crossed the $50 million annual revenue barrier, as opposed to only 144 nonprofits. That's shocking. The most effective and economical way to solve big problems is not 10,000 organizations serving 100 people per year, but rather 100 operationally and programmatically excellent organizations each serving 10,000."

We need more nonprofits to take the passion, tell the compelling narrative, think out of the box, set a great vision and want to go big in order to make a greater impact. Again, yes, we need the small local charities, but we need more nonprofits to grow to a larger scale in order to touch more lives.

We need to assure the public trust remains fully in tact for nonprofits to demonstrate that they can substantially address the challenges in society, with passion and business sense. More need to expand in a way that can be replicated or is scalable.

And, today, we need to ensure that nonprofits are positioned to partner and be sufficiently able to compete for resources with their for-profit counterparts. These for-profit organizations will not be going away, but rather will be challenging the sector to become more business oriented, capitalistic and efficient.

Ultimately, we need more nonprofits to go big, gain a lot of trust equity, make impact and grow (serve more) or go home.

2   "The New Nonprofit IPO," Stanford Social Innovation Review, January 29, 2014, http://www.ssireview.org/blog/entry/the_new_nonprofit_ipo

FOUR
Go Big or Go Home

Corporate Funder: Sometimes I wonder, Wayne, what some nonprofits are thinking. I have organizations send me reams and reams of paper as if I am going to sit and sort through their mess. It's pretty easy for me to know whom I am going to seriously consider and whom I am going to toss to the side with a letter of regret.

We have fluctuated between 1.5 million and as high as 1.8 million nonprofits in the United States. As I mentioned in the previous chapter, since 1970 only 144 nonprofits have crossed the $50 million revenue mark as compared to 46,000 for-profit businesses. In today's environment, that is not acceptable.

We know that the larger an organization becomes, the lower cost per unit to deliver services or products. We also know that big companies have the benefit of convincing start-up businesses to sell to them for increased market share, expansion capital and access to excellent personnel. Therefore, we do need more nonprofits growing larger.

However, I also understand three salient points about small organizations. First, most nonprofits that become large were once small start-up operations. Second, while it is important for more nonprofits to grow larger in order to leverage resources, there is still room for the small mom and pop organizations. These small entities tend know their local market well and are able to respond quickly because they lack bureaucracy. Third, even if a nonprofit remains small, every organization should have **big vision**. Anything less is not acceptable.

Nonprofits are the ones in need of the **best** talent, marketing, strategy consulting, fundraising technology and expertise, infrastructure, etc. because these organizations seek to change society and impact lives.

Still, donors and philanthropic supporters are beyond the days when they were content with 15 charities in the same town doing the same thing and each helping 100 people. Is there way to partner with each other, leverage resources and, in some cases, consolidate? I think so.

A friend told me one time that she was looking to support music education for children. She did a Google search and thought she would find one or two organizations she could support. She was surprised when she was faced with more than two-dozen organizations in her city.

She went a little further and realized that many of these nonprofits were established and were clearly languishing offering programs to a handful of children. She wondered why these organizations could not consolidate or merge and leverage greater resources. I agree. It seems pretty impractical to keep perpetuating more of the same.

By leveraging resources, by growing and tackling problems with a lot of "fire power," not just money, but also intellectual knowledge, I think we can really make momentous changes today. We shouldn't be satisfied with just creating more nonprofits that mean well but will likely remain small and only address a small sliver of the population.

If we start to think big and if we start to go big, we can make significant changes. We can leverage resources of money, momentum, donor support, technology, and intellectual property and make a marked change.

Yes, it's always important to save one life. But, what if we can strategically combine resources and save 1 million lives? Just like Dan Duffy is thinking. He started with 700 pairs of shoes … in theory, 700 lives. Now, he's going for 1 million.

The problems that society has to deal with around poverty, justice, income inequality, work opportunities, education, environment, health, etc., have been seemingly incurable since the beginning of any time. Today, we definitely have the resources, if we combined and multiplied our efforts, to eradicate many of these issues.

We know, for example, that we most definitely produce enough food to feed the world. We know that. It's a fact. Yet, tens of millions of children die each year for lack of nutritious food. That's simply unacceptable.

But many of us don't believe that we are just going to have to live with these challenges in perpetuity. Let me provide you with a concrete example.

Gates And The End of Malaria

Bill Gates has publicly stated and is actively working, along with his wife and partner, Melinda Gates, and their team on the eradication of malaria. In November 2014 he stated in his blog that from what he was seeing malaria would be cured "in every country–within a generation."

Melinda Gates made comments that are even more compelling, "Any goal short of eradicating malaria is accepting malaria; it's making peace with malaria; it's rich countries saying: 'We don't need to eradicate malaria around the world as long as we've eliminated malaria in our own countries.' That's just unacceptable."

That's certainly an audacious goal and I am sure somewhere in the world there is someone who is saying the eradication of this disease is impossible. But, the thought leadership, and the very audacity of that vision is exactly what today's philanthropists are looking for in order to truly change the world.

And, with clear minded focus and investment on the pursuit of that goal, Bill and Melinda Gates have enabled scientists and humanitarians to eliminate malaria in four countries since 2000, and with his projection that this will too be the case in more than two-dozen countries in the next decade, they continue to work toward the end goal.

Just so you know, the parasite that is responsible for malaria has been in existence for tens of thousands of years. References to it can be found as far back as 2700 B.C. in China.

What if Bill and Melinda Gates simply thought that since malaria has been around for centuries and millennia that it was simply too complex a scientific problem to every really truly solve?

Well, for starters, 3.3 million people would not be alive today.

Almost Isn't Good Enough

Today's donors–big and small–visionaries and leaders do not find it okay to simply continue with the same business as usual. They want to see measurable change occur within organizations that address any of these challenges, and more. They want to see organizations that are transparent, accountable and responsive to their needs as donors and the needs of those being served by the nonprofit.

They want to see big things happen and are not satisfied with a vision that will "almost" solve the problem. ***Almost isn't good enough***.

This desire is being fueled by the inordinate success people are seeing in the corporate sector. If you look at for-profit and nonprofit businesses, you will see that today's leaders are being created and brought into the public arena at unprecedented levels. Enormous success and incredible wealth are being brought to bear to the people associated with these enterprises within a very small timeframe.

Gone are the days when people built up businesses, or nonprofits, and slowly grew them over the course of 3, 5 or 10 years. Because of the enormous troves of information we all have at our fingertips, we know people around the world are crushing it. We know what success looks like and we know the "impossible" is possible.

Dan and Teri make it a personal mission to do so much more than folks they may have met along their respective paths ever thought possible. So too there are businesses, social enterprises and nonprofits, which have started from nothing to become powerhouses. These organizations do what others thought was the improbable, if not impossible, in short order.

Businesses that have blasted into unprecedented levels of success include Apple, Amazon, Google, Netflix, Airbnb and Uber.

The same can be said of the following top social enterprises, which can encompass nonprofits or for-profit hybrids, such as Kiva, TOMS, KIPP Foundation, Opower, Grameen Bank, Room to Read and Ashoka: Innovators for the Public, Teach for America and Susan G. Komen for the Cure.

The list goes on!

All of their leaders laid out a great vision—a big vision—and they worked to make it happen. Always staying ahead of the curve and adapting to the changing business, economic, social and global landscape.

Mark Zuckerberg of Facebook is a Millennial who ushered in the world in social media. Now that his company has matured, he is not satisfied. He now has the goal of bringing the Internet to the two-thirds of the world population that live in circumstances that are so impoverished or rural that they have no access to the digital world.

He helped establish Internet.org, which is creating partnerships between leaders in technology, nonprofits and local communities around the world to provide every person on this planet with Internet access.

Zuckerberg just turned 30 and he already has experienced such enormous success and conquered what would have taken a lifetime for others to do. This is a whole new world.

The Rise and Fail of Charities and What You Can Do To Be Ready
Wayne Elsey

Why is this possible? The answer is technology and scientific advances are happening at lightening speed. And, this era is here to stay.

In order to be able to get an education, find work opportunities that may not exist in a local community or country, to help propel human progress forward, you need people who can access information and communicate across town or around the world efficiently and instantaneously.

It's happening now. Big vision = Global change.

If every person on earth has access to a mobile device, in addition to education and work opportunities, it changes lives. People will have access, for example, to online banking (in other words, they don't have to walk miles to pay debts or obtain money). They will be empowered to do banking in ways they had never been able to do before making for easier commerce and higher living standards.

I think it is fair to say that if I asked any leader who is thinking big if they thought what they were doing was impossible, I would receive a resounding "no." Why bother to get in the game if you think you are going to lose? Why bother to try if you think you can't make it happen?

Funds2Orgs And My Work

At this point, if I were you, I would ask me, "Well, Wayne, what are you doing that makes you such an expert and what is your big idea?"

"Sure, let me explain."

For those of you who do not know how I got started working in the nonprofit sector and social enterprise, a brief history. When the 2004 Indian Ocean tsunami struck, I was stunned by the vast amount of devastation and the lives lost, as was much of the world. It was an incredibly profound event in our world history.

On the television screen one night, I saw a single shoe wash ashore.

At that point, I was a very successful executive in the shoe business working at an international scale. That shoe and everything it represented of the loss of life stayed with me. It was profound and it was something that I couldn't shake from my mind.

Within days I decided to do something. Using every possible contact I had in the shoe industry, I led the charge to provide hundreds of thousands of shoes to the countries that were affected. The need for every single necessity was so overwhelming, and this included shoes.

Within a few short years, I established the Soles4Souls nonprofit organization and in less than 5 years took it from zero dollars in revenue to over $70 million. Anyone can do this and nonprofits need to internalize that message.

I will tell you that there was controversy throughout my tenure, which is a matter of public record. But, this ended up being a blessing in disguise. I came to crystallize my thinking around the fact that I am someone who is exceedingly entrepreneurial and I have a passion for starting new businesses.

For the sake of transparency, if you are interested in some of the past background of my professional career, feel free to research it on the Internet. While you're at it, definitely please take a look at my response to my critics regarding my tenure at Soles4Souls on my blog Not Your Father's Charity.[3]

Since that time, I established *Wayne Elsey Enterprises* with several subsidiary brands:

- *str@tegic* – focusing on leadership and business strategy.

- *Funds2Orgs* – a social enterprise that enables individuals, companies and organizations to raise funds while helping to support micro-enterprise opportunities in developing nations.

- *501C3U* – a free online university for nonprofit education.

- *Not Your Father's Charity (NYFC)* – my blog and a forum that enables social entrepreneurs, philanthropists, nonprofits, the media and general public to learn how to succeed in 21st Century social enterprise.

I love all the work we do. Funds2Orgs is special because it's my social enterprise. I have the chance to make positive social change in places such as Haiti, Tanzania and Guatemala. My team and I also help the environment. And, we provide nonprofits and charitable organizations in the United States and abroad with a unique, fun and easy fundraising opportunity that helps raise their brand's visibility. There are so many more benefits to these nonprofits beyond just their organization.

Allow me to provide you with a very specific example of my work in Haiti, for example.

When Haiti suffered its devastating 7.0 magnitude earthquake on January 12, 2010, I again found myself feeling the urgent call to action that I felt follow-

---

3   "Response to the Tennessean Article from Soles4Souls," Not Your Father's Charity, April 4, 2011, http://notyourfatherscharity.com/response-tennessean-article-soles4souls/

ing the Indian Ocean tsunami.

Haiti is an impoverished country of fewer than 10 million people. And on the day of the earthquake, 300,000 lost their lives and an additional 300,000 were injured with 1.5 million left homeless. The damages were over $7.8 billion.

It has taken years to get the country where the average wage, as a reminder, is $2 a day to where they were on January 11, 2010–the day before the country was crushed with the quake. Mind you, the world has advanced leaps and bounds ahead in the five years since the earthquake.

I have taken a special interest in Haiti and by extension, so has Funds2Orgs. I firmly believe that we need to provide people in developing nations with opportunities for work, education and learning. It is not sufficient to simply give them food or shelter. Charity helps cure the unsteadiness for a day, but it is philanthropy, which enables people to fend for themselves.

Exactly 5 years to the day after the earthquake, Funds2Orgs opened its first micro-enterprise training depot in Port-au-Prince, Haiti. The training depot was created to serve as a center for learning and education for budding entrepreneurs in Haiti where poverty is so devastating that work opportunities are scarce. The bottom line is that the best way for the people of Haiti to find their way out of poverty is to create their own opportunity. And, that is what Funds2Orgs is doing for them.

It is providing entrepreneurs the resources and skills so they can create their own small "micro-businesses." These micro-businesses are typically small operations that are operated by a handful of people, usually family members. Funds2Orgs has been operating in Haiti for a number of years and it has helped small business owners go from earning $2 a day to over $60.

For the sake of clarity, Funds2Orgs partners with business, corporations, nonprofit organizations such as schools, youth sports teams, church congregations and others to collect shoes from their respective communities.

This is a win/win because as I explained in the previous chapter with Dan Duffy's organization, the sponsoring organization for the shoe drive is paid based on the quantity of shoes collected. More shoes = More money.

Those shoes are consolidated and then shipped to developing nations such as Haiti, Tanzania and Guatemala. Once in those countries, Funds2Orgs works with small hub distributors there who purchase the shoes for pennies on the dollar. They then re-sell them to small micro-entrepreneurs. Finally, the repurposed shoes (i.e. cleaned and made to look like new) are sold to customers for a profit by these micro-entrepreneurs.

At no cost, the Funds2Orgs Micro-Enterprise Training Depot offers courses in math, reading and writing and helps enrolled participants develop basic business skills. Students are required to attend classes in order to successfully complete the program and they are incentivized with future discounts on inventory. With only just over half of the adult population having an elementary education, these skills are essential in order for them to become successful in developing their small businesses.

Funds2Orgs is also the supplier to these new entrepreneurs and provides them, for free, with the initial inventory they need to sell, including sneakers, shoes, clothing, purses and cell phone chargers. Future inventory is purchased from the profits the micro-entrepreneurs will be making.

My team and I envision the Funds2Orgs Micro-Enterprise Training Depot in Port-au-Prince, Haiti to be the first training center of others that will be established in time in other parts of Haiti and in other developing countries.

But Funds2Orgs and I are not the only ones thinking big and working to develop new and innovative ways to philanthropically diminish, if not completely eradicate, many of society's challenges that have been with us from one generation to the next.

Big Is Good

Leading organizations truly believe in "going big or going home" and it does not only mean having to go big on scale (growth). Not every nonprofit has a necessity to go global, even though every nonprofit should be locally *and* globally aware. Not every nonprofit may even have a need to go national, or even citywide. But, every nonprofit should set its sights on a big vision and "going big" certainly means big impact and results. Going big also means *constantly* evolving and innovating in a world that requires it at every level.

Going big means not showing up with the tin cup mentality and looking at your nonprofit organization through a 20th Century lens. Many of the old ways of doing business simply do not apply anymore, although I do believe some "old school" principles do still apply, such as personal communication.

Going big means looking to make the deepest and broadest impact your organization can make and it means letting go of the pessimistic thinking. This old time thinking dictates that we need to live with things as they are because "things never change."

Going big means *never* accepting, "we've always done it that way," when things can clearly be improved or done more efficiently and effectively.

There are many great nonprofits, large and small, that are thought leaders

The Rise and Fail of Charities and What You Can Do To Be Ready
Wayne Elsey

and have broken with the old polyester paradigm of existence. But, from time to time I have the opportunity to highlight a few leading examples. Here are some nonprofit organizations that are going big, and in my mind are leading the way with regard to vision, impact and innovation:

- **Donorschoose.org** – I think no matter what side of the political aisle you are on, we can agree that we need to improve education. Government cutbacks have cut into necessary resources for schools and children are always on the losing end of that approach. DonorsChoose.org is an online organization that enables anyone to help students through crowd funding. Public schools teachers post classroom requests on the site and the amount they need. Donors then help fund the request and when the goal is reached, the materials are shipped. Donors then receive photos, a letter from the teacher and are informed about "how every dollar was spent." To date, they have raised over $306 million, helped over 13.9 million children and funded over 549,000 projects. Oh, and by the way, this organization was only established 15 years ago.

- **DoSomething.org** – This is one of my favorite organizations because it motivates young people to, well, do something and "make the world suck less." It is one of the largest organizations for the young and social change with 3.3 million members that work on "any cause, anytime, anywhere." But, what is interesting about this nonprofit is that 10 years after it was established, it almost imploded. The current CEO, Nancy Lublin, began to lead the organization after they had just let go of 21 of 22 people on staff. They had $75,000 remaining in the bank and were $250,000 in debt. She made a bet on closing down any remaining office space and relying on the Internet, and almost lost her job because the board thought it was too risky. The bet paid off, and last year, they had 50 full-time employees and were more than back on track doing their youth campaigns.

- **Room to Read** – This organization was founded in 2000 and is seeking to ensure a quality education for all children. The way it accomplishes its mission is to focus on two key areas: literacy and gender equality in education. In 2013, they raised over $41.6 million in cash donations with an additional $6.3 million in in-kind donations. They have established over 17,000 libraries, constructed over 1,800 schools, distributed over $14.5 million books and benefited over 8.8 million children in Asia and Africa. In my opinion, Room to Read also happens to have one of the clearest websites that I have seen for a nonprofit, which communicates what they are doing, the impact they are having in an extremely easy to navigate manner. All nonprofits should strive to present themselves publicly as well as this organization does.

- **CaringBridge** – Sona Mehring, who had previously led a firm, which developed websites, established this Internet based nonprofit in 1997. As she succinctly explains on the site, "In 1997, good friends of mine had a premature baby, and they asked me to let everyone know what was happening. Instead of making dozens of emotional and time-consuming phone calls, I decided to create a website. The same night their baby Brighid was born so was the idea that became CaringBridge." Over 500,000 people a day use the caring bridge website by creating and updating their own web pages to update and communicate, in a privately created space, with their followers when they are most in need of support. They have over 2,500 volunteers and if you check them out, you will see that they leverage the Internet in every way possible because they understand that people are global and mobile and they need to access information how and when they want and need it.

- **Teach For America** – Harvard Business School has written four case studies about this socially innovative nonprofit. The organization, whose mission is to "eliminate educational inequity by enlisting high-achieving recent college graduates and professionals to teach" was founded in 1989. Its most recent financials show its revenue exceeds over $276 million. If you even take a cursory look at their website, you will see they speak about "investment" and they know how to communicate with the general public about what is rolled up into their revenue numbers. With that, they are able to serve 10,600 active classroom teachers throughout the country and over 37,000 alumni.

Going big, in some way that is relevant to them, is something every non-profit organization should be thinking and doing.

The Rise and Fail of Charities and What You Can Do To Be Ready
Wayne Elsey

FIVE
Money, Money, Money

Individual Donor: I received a year-end bonus and I was feeling pretty good. I wanted to give some money to my kid's school and I went online to quickly make a gift while I was riding in the back of a cab. The school didn't have a donation page. Then I thought they'll just get me when they ask for money, but by then I probably won't be giving what I would have given today.

Money is like gold.

If you are a nonprofit executive or board member who spends his or her time fundraising, I think you probably agree. It is precious and it takes work (and risk) to earn it.

I have written about this in the past, and it's important to write about it in the context of this book. It's a key reason it may make nonprofits great or perpetual failures going from one crisis to the next.

Aside from the right leadership that brings forward the great vision and the trust capital, the lack of deep conversation within a nonprofit about money is counterproductive and dangerous to the sustainability of any organization.

In my opinion, one of the most difficult conversations that nonprofits need to be having revolves around money. Yes, most people get into the nonprofit sector because they want to make an impact in society. That is all well and good, but money makes the world go 'round. You can't run away or hide from that fact.

I have been the founder of a nonprofit and in my current life each day I wake up as a social entrepreneur and business owner and speak to nonprofit executives. I still find many nonprofit executives to be timid or too conservative when speaking about money. I also find executives who use words of "hope" and "we'll see" when it comes to donors making donations to their organizations. Those words do not inspire great confidence and commitment to the plan, whatever it is.

One of the biggest complaints I hear from nonprofit executives is that it is very difficult for them to get donors to give. They worry about ongoing support. And, yet, when I probe a little further on that question, I find out oftentimes they are too timid to ask and they definitely don't like to ask more than once.

Where's the conversation about money? If nonprofit leaders are not doing it each and every day, when will they be doing it?

A nonprofit executive might ask once, not get the response he or she anticipated and decide to not ask again until next year. I have seen this happen time and time again.

There's an old adage in sales, each "no" is one step closer to a "yes." By asking probing questions, you find out what it will take for someone to support your organization.

We know that there is a scarcity of top-of-the-line fundraisers, and they typically stay in any position no more than two years. This is one of the reasons why: they are good because they know how to ask for money. They are not afraid to ask for money. They are "closers" and the best nonprofits want these professionals on their teams.

Donors want to help you and they want to invest in your organization—especially if they see energy and momentum that are making an impact. Savvy donors understand that money is the lifeblood to a successful enterprise and they understand you need to ask.

Sometimes I sit with executives and I ask questions about average gift, ROI or what areas they need for the biggest investments and why. I may ask about a reserve fund or projections they might have going out one to three years. Too often I see the CEO of a nonprofit defer these questions to the CFO or COO when he or she should be very well versed and comfortable speaking about the money. This is a shame and it does not do the organization—or the executive—justice.

Yes, nonprofits need to be mindful of the money they receive through donations and they have a special obligation to be transparent and not wasteful. I

The Rise and Fail of Charities and What You Can Do To Be Ready
Wayne Elsey

do understand that. But it is in their best interest for executives to become very comfortable in talking about money for their own sakes.

Let me make a simple example. If you went to work each week and at the end of the pay period you were not paid, wouldn't you say something?

I imagine you have bills to pay. You may have rent or a mortgage. You need to put gas in the car. You need to pay for groceries and the light bill at home. You may have children and need to spend a whole lot of money there to keep them clothed, well fed and educated. I am sure if you were working and were not getting paid, you would say something.

Well, just as you would say something for yourself, you need to be able to speak up for your nonprofit. Donors will continue to give **much less** than they could potentially give if they remain uninformed about what you are doing, what you need, why you need it, your results and why it matters.

Donors will continue to want to direct their money toward only program expenses as opposed to providing for administrative overhead as long as non-profit executives continue to avoid the conversation. Nonprofits will remain treading water as opposed to taking a certain amount of calculated risk on investment in order to see returns in a new revenue stream.

One Side Of The Coin

I have spoken to fundraising consultants, in particular, who tell me they have nonprofits that reach out to them on a regular basis asking for help. They know they want to diversify their income, or they want to focus on establishing a major gifts program. But, when the time comes to talk about money, they don't want to make the necessary investment.

And, if they do pay, they don't make the long-term commitment. In other words, if they don't see money come in from major donors within three months, for example, they fire the consultant and go back to business as usual. If anyone has ever worked with major donors, especially cold prospects, you know three months is nowhere near enough time. Can you really establish a re-lationship, cultivate them and then make an ask that closes for five, six or even seven figures within three months? Sure, anything is possible, but this is not likely. On average, those sorts of gifts take at least six months, or more, to close.

You find nonprofit executives who ask outsiders for help on a percentage basis, even though this is plainly unethical based on the norms and practices of the Association of Fundraising Professionals. Or, they ask anyone and every-one to simply volunteer their time.

I have heard situations where individuals have provided an expertise on a pro bono basis only to have a nonprofit take advantage of them, which simply fosters resentment and ill will.

Why are nonprofits always looking for the low cost or free option? The reason is because money is always an issue. Much more of an issue than it needs to be.

If every nonprofit executive became eloquent speaking about the elephant in the room, it would serve their organization so much better.

Aversion to risk often makes organizations dip a toe in the water and then immediately take it out because it is too cold, even though the right strategy would be to dive right in and start to swim.

There is another side to that same coin of fear of money.

And, The Other Side Of The Coin

We call on nonprofit organizations every day for Funds2Orgs in particular. I have a great team that works with me and there is no way we could be as successful as we are without the contributions of the staff.

Those of us who are on the sales side of the business, love selling to schools, nonprofits and youth sports organizations, among others. More importantly, we know we are providing an opportunity to have nonprofits participate in a fun and easy fundraiser–with no cost to them upfront.

Donors are able to accomplish all of the following:
- Support their local nonprofit.
- Clear out their closets of shoes and sneakers that are only taking up space.
- Save the environment from more unnecessary and unhealthy refuse with these items being thrown into landfills.
- Help support micro-enterprise.

My social enterprise is a leader in this type of fundraising. We are not a "fly-by-night" and we are highly networked into the business and nonprofit sector. I have been featured on television and national business magazines. We have a brick and mortar office; we work locally in Florida where our headquarters is based, across the nation and internationally.

So, why I am telling you all this?

Day in and day out, I have nonprofits that love what they hear from me who then question me about *not* having to make any upfront investment.

Huh?

"Where's the catch?" the nonprofit executive will say to me.

There is no catch, and unfortunately every day we discontinue conversations with organization (many who originally sought us out) simply because they can't believe they have to make *no* upfront investment. They have a big fear that there is some catch they are missing and they will actually end up losing money rather than gaining money.

It's just fear, fear, and fear.

Here's the thing. We do make money, but not from nonprofits.

We have a business model whereby we are able to essentially purchase the shoes collected from a nonprofit and pay the organization for their excellent efforts by following our plan. We then make money on the business partnerships we have with our micro-entrepreneurs who are growing their own businesses in developing nations.

So, it's kind of ironic, when you think about it. I have consulting colleagues in the field who are regularly sought out to provide their experience and expertise for *free* because nonprofits say they have no money. However, when I offer them a way to raise revenue with *no* upfront costs, they can't believe it and are too afraid.

It's an unhealthy cycle of not being comfortable about talking and dealing with money and subconsciously always existing in some sort of crisis mode. In order for today's nonprofits to make a measurable impact and go beyond treading water, this has to end.

Why The Money Talk?

Nonprofits need to go beyond struggling for small victories and they have to become well versed in money.

Why?

- **Money is measurable** – What you see is what you get with money. Money can be reviewed and analyzed to the penny. There is no ambiguity about how much money you have in the bank, and if you have more expenses than money in the bank, you know you will be running at a deficit. Money provides you with a tool of information that helps you make informed decisions. In other words, if you are looking to expand a certain area of your nonprofit and it will take $100,000, you know that you need to have that money in the bank or you will have to raise it via a loan, fundraising or investment capital.

- **Money marks engagement** – Money is fluid and it is constantly being received and spent. If you are talking about money in the nonprofit sector, it means you have engaged someone. You have interested them enough that you think the time has come to speak about money. And, if they are supporting your organization, it means you have moved them to take action. If you are very good at what you do, you help support and encourage your donors to become advocates and ambassadors for your organization and tell others in their sphere of influence to support you.

- **Money builds capacity** – There is no way of getting around it. Money for programs is essential, but so is money for paying the best people in the field to come and work for your organization. Money is needed for the space you rent, the utility bills and the computers and technical devices you need to use in today's environment. Taking a tablet device to a major donor meeting does not mean you are being wasteful. On the contrary. Investing in this shows you know how to use technology to your benefit and you are not cutting trees that have no need to be destroyed for printing proposals and collateral material that will only be skimmed through and put to the side never to be seen again.

- **Money means accountability** - Anyone who donates to a nonprofit wants transparency and accountability. In addition, the government is looking to make sure there are legal and fiduciary accountabilities, as well as the media and general public. When individuals, foundations, trusts, government (tax payer money) or corporations give to an organization, they expect that the money will be expensed in a responsible manner which allows the organization to further its mission and work. Gone are the days when donors would give to an organization and expect to hear from them sometime the following year. Today's donor and even the public want to make sure every nonprofit that is benefiting from that tax status is behaving responsibly, engaging with others and holding themselves out to be accountable for how the monies are spent in relation to the work being done. That is why we see every year articles written about scam nonprofits. These scammers are a stain on the trust capital that the nonprofit sector needs to effectively and transparently work.

The Rise and Fail of Charities and What You Can Do To Be Ready
Wayne Elsey

- **Money forces tough decisions** – It is very simple. If there is no money to do what you need to do, you can't do it. When nonprofits are failing, money forces them to sometimes take drastic steps. It means having to cut into operating revenue and then, ultimately, into programs, which is something no nonprofit ever wants to do because it cuts into their mission. But this fact is actually a good thing for nonprofits because it forces executives and board members to constantly prioritize what it is they are seeking to do. Excellent executives are able to see that money is a great check for reflecting on the past, present and future of an organization in order to make wise decisions.

- **Money forces innovation, if you can see the opportunity** – Many nonprofits operate in a never-ending state of crisis. I read one time how nonprofits don't usually like to hire people who have experience wholly from the corporate sector because they don't understand this "crisis mentality." These professionals get tired and they tend to go back into the corporate sector where there is money. This, in my opinion, if true is obviously a mistake. Nonprofits need to be bringing in and recruiting people not just with solid nonprofit experience, but also with corporate experience. Organizations should be looking to expand and be open to finding innovative and different roads than they have tried in the past to execute programs or raise capital. This means working with people with diverse backgrounds and experience. It also means not leaning on the old fundraising rulebook.

The Starvation Cycle

While I believe that too many nonprofit executives are too timid when speaking about money, I also think that donors bear a certain amount of responsibility as well for the nonprofit starvation cycle in which many organizations find themselves.

The starvation cycle, simply, is a never-ending cycle where nonprofits are unable to secure the sufficient amount of investment money they need to operate effectively. The reason for this is because donors have unrealistic expectations about what it takes for a nonprofit business to exist.

Donors prefer to give money directly to program costs and they would rather not pay for the rent, research and development, professional development and expertise, utility bills. Given the choice, donors would rather not support the necessary administrative and operational infrastructure that a business needs to operate.

In turn, you have a sort of game being played with nonprofit organizations moving money around to make sure they keep their operating expense ratios as unrealistically low as possible.

I'm **not** saying they are doing anything illegal.

Of course, most nonprofits are not doing anything illegal. There are fail-safes in place to make sure nonprofits are accountable with the IRS filings that need to happen and audited financials (for those nonprofits with large enough budgets) that need to be filed. Additionally, corporations and foundations tend to only fund charitable organizations that have an independent certified public accountant review their books on an annual basis.

However, what does happen is that nonprofit executives may place some of the money that in all reality should be in operating expenditures instead in program costs. This then skews a nonprofit's true operating costs and organizational effectiveness. It's a dirty little secret that exists in the sector, which shouldn't.

So, donors need to be reminded or educated around the fact that *a nonprofit is a business*. Being designated, as a "nonprofit" organization is only for tax purposes and it is not a business model.

Nonprofit organizations need to be liberated from their perpetual second-class citizen status. Executives and board members need to become effective and well versed in speaking about money.

They need to first understand for themselves, and wholly believe, that they are running a business. And, as such, they are looking to make a lot of revenue so they can then reinvest that money, instead of distributing it to shareholders. This ensures that they are able to have the necessary resources to secure the organization's success. As a matter of fact, this is an obligation and duty of nonprofit executives and board members.

Once this occurs at a leadership level, money and its true relationship to the nonprofit organization needs to be communicated to the general public, repeatedly.

The general public and donors need to understand that their money is necessary and crucial to pay the administrative and operational bills, which are the underpinning foundation of the business. Of course, money is also required for programs, which are obviously the heart of the mission. But the mission cannot be fully accomplished without *investment* into the operating costs of the business.

Nonprofits need to stop being okay with operating in a state of perpetual crisis. This permeates the industry and it results in our colleagues and friends who are consultants and excellent professionals from being paid a competitive salary. It filters down from the top to junior level staff who are expected to have invested in their own educations.

In this day and age young workers may have college debt to the tune of $30,000 to $40,000 only to then earn $18,000 or $20,000 a year working full-time at a nonprofit. We need to end the expectation by nonprofits that they have to pay workers as little as possible–or have them work as volunteers–but expect top credentials and a high level of experience. One does not go with the other.

Nonprofits should **not** be having a conversation with donors about how **little** they are spending. They should instead be speaking to them about how **much** impact they are having relative to their budget. Nonprofits should be looking to make a lot of money, just as capitalist businesses do, because that money will only be reinvested, in whole, right back into its successful business.

It should not be a badge of honor to be proud of operating on a shoestring budget. It should not be acceptable to state your operating expenses are only 5 percent or even 0 percent of your overall budget. Any for-profit executive who dared to say that to investors or his or her board would be laughed right out of the boardroom.

We know that 0 percent overhead cost is not accurate or even possible.

We know that is moving money from one line item to another only skews an organization's true effectiveness and that of the industry as a whole. Funders come to believe that great things can happen with 0 percent operating costs, when that is not realistic.

It's just playing right into the myth.

And this brings me right back to my two main points. All of this,

1) Breeds a lack of trust and the loss of trust capital; and,

2) It provides a very good opening for others to claim that nonprofits have had their chance and they can do it better.

If you have not realized, a conversation has already begun about social enterprises that operate as sort of hybrid organizations and corporations to fill in the space where nonprofits are seemingly failing.

But, many nonprofits are failing not because they have wanted to fail or they are not interested in outcomes. On the contrary, I think most nonprofit professionals really care about making a large impact as it relates to their mission.

However, many are failing because there is a growing buzz and conversation happening in the general public about investment capital infusing the nonprofit sector, *or not*, and making great impact and social change. There are now alternatives to nonprofits.

Nonprofit professionals and those who care about the sector need to be thought leaders in this space. The reality is it is going to take a partnership between government, corporations, businesses and nonprofits. For-profits are definitely capable of making a societal impact, but they are beholden to their shareholders, not to society, as are nonprofits. These partnerships are already beginning to take place with forward thinking nonprofit organizations that do not want be rendered obsolete.

Thus, an earnest education process and ongoing conversations need to take place so that funders are slowly re-educated to think how they look at evaluating nonprofits. Nonprofit leaders need to become well versed in business practices, and I am a big proponent of for-profit entrepreneurs and MBA's entering the space.

The general public and donors need to be comfortable talking about money and not looking at nonprofits as if they are not serious businesses where investment capital is required.

SIX

The Nonprofit Leader of Today

Ex-Nonprofit Board Member: I was asked to volunteer for this small international nonprofit. I happen to have expertise, 20 years, in the field. They thought I would be a good addition. It was a total waste of time and I resigned within three months. Total disorganization, lack of strategy and vision and just going from one crisis to another. Who has time for that?

There is sometimes a debate about whether nonprofits and social enterprises are one in the same. Different countries sometimes have differing interpretations.

Yes, certainly, there are social enterprises that are leading nonprofit organizations because of their particular tax designation by the Internal Revenue Service in the United States. However, there are social enterprises that are for-profit businesses.

Social enterprises, either for-profit or nonprofit, seek innovative solutions to solve the societal issues that challenge society. Performance metrics always include their impact on society as it relates to the social mission of the organization.

There is one important nuance that I think differentiates many social entrepreneurs and nonprofits. Social entrepreneurs tend to infuse more for-profit business practices into their organizations and nonprofits have a leaning to traditional methods to operate.

Historically, nonprofits relied on the social contract where there was a belief that people wanted to "make a difference" and the organization would obtain money from donors to help accomplish their mission.

As I have highlighted in this book, all of this is changing. Funders are no longer interested in perpetually funding programs that are not making a verifiable and measurable impact. They are demanding a return on investment by requiring nonprofit organizations to demonstrate measurable results and impact. They want evidence of change.

As a matter of fact "make a difference" is such a cliché now because it has to really have meaning. People are more comfortable with dialogue about "impact."

Social enterprises, a relatively new concept marrying the best practices of the nonprofit and for-profit sectors, are more inclined to use solid business principles. It is much more common to hear social entrepreneur leaders speak of ROI and investment, for example, than it is to hear a nonprofit leader.

Since social entrepreneurs look to for-profit principles, especially if they are a for-profit venture, they understand calculated risks. They are not timid to try new things.

As these enterprises seek solutions to address the societal issues they would like to impact, they look to creative methods–perhaps never tried before–to see if they could significantly impact and change for the better the intractable challenges in society.

I think any organization runs the risk of inertia or maintaining of the status quo. Humans tend to be creatures of habit and change is sometimes very challenging. It is natural to want to avoid the pain and "if it ain't broke, don't fix it."

But, any company, social enterprise or nonprofit that thinks it can stay relevant with yesterday's methods and approaches is making a mistake. It is setting itself up for failure and it is squandering any trust capital that it may have built through the years.

Every successful nonprofit executive is continually looking at how to approach donors in their 20's to those in their 80's. Top fundraisers and executives are always looking at how to connect and encourage donors–government, individuals, corporations or foundations–to continue to support their efforts. This means, leading nonprofit executives understand that no single approach will work for every donor prospect. They understand they must be creative and flexible and they need to address the multiple needs of their donors.

In today's chaotic and innovative business environment due to globalization and enormous advances in science and technology, this means that in order to develop and retain trust capital from supporters, leaders need to be looking to evolve. In addition, as these leaders grow, they must also lead their organizations in becoming accustomed to adapting to ongoing changes.

Leaders, like the organizations they serve, need to be forward thinking and they need to have qualities that help inspire success under a new global paradigm of success. Nonprofit leaders need to have a high degree of ethics and integrity, especially because in the United States, they lead organizations that are tax exempt.

Today's leadership also means these leaders, and their social purpose entities have a special obligation to the tax paying public. It requires a high level of transparency, which helps to build and sustain trust capital not only for a specific organization but also for the industry as a whole.

Leadership is something that continually needs to be developed and refined. One of the most powerful an all encompassing thoughts about the qualities and characteristics I have ever read about leadership were written by John Kotter, a Harvard professor, in his book, "Leading Change."

In the book, he spoke about dissatisfaction. Essentially, he said, leaders need to be *dissatisfied* with the way things are in the present. They need to be dissatisfied with what exists and set out to improve, which means they also have to have a clear vision for how things should be done and, finally, they need to know how to start to get there.

Although the book was written in the latter part of the last century, those elements are still very much true and they are probably even more valid today than on the day they were published.

A leader, particularly in today's world, needs to know and understand how things can be done better. He or she needs to have the vision for a better way of improving and doing things and the leader needs to have a rough idea of how to get there. From there, everything else will follow.

I've often said I think many nonprofit professionals today still rely on the old school ways and methods. They rely on successes of the past and many are not leading change. There is a timidity that permeates through the sector and prevents creativity and innovation from taking a hold in each and every single nonprofit.

Although there are thought leaders and innovators taking their nonprofits from zero to multi-million organizations and operating at scale, there are still *so* many that flounder year after year. And, again, this helps diminish trust capital in the nonprofit sector and provides opportunity for others, in particular for-profit social enterprises or companies.

If things continue with many nonprofit organizations staying static and adhering to the status quo, I can envision a future where the conversation will increasingly be with stakeholders that do not include many in the nonprofit industry.

And, with that, donors will also be taking their money and providing it to organizations that can address their requirements for a high-level of transparency, results and measurable impact. They're not going to care if they are for-profit social enterprises or even companies. They just want to see the change and social good happen.

I think a lot of it has to with a history within the nonprofit sector to be risk averse and maintain the status quo. Additionally, I have seen too many leaders who are timid about bold leadership and do not want to rock the proverbial boat.

Yes, a certain degree of prudence and pragmatism are important, but true leadership rewards those who are have gone against the grain. True leadership rewards those who have big vision and can inspire people to follow. It rewards those who have been dissatisfied at the way things were and decided that in order to improve conditions, they needed to create a new dynamic or change the conversation.

Throughout business, we have seen this demonstrated time and again. My three favorite are Bill and Melinda Gates and Steve Jobs: all brilliant, bold, visionary, decisive and unrelenting leaders. They were not satisfied.

Bill and Melinda Gates – Bill Gates is known as the founder Microsoft and with Steve Jobs, the co-founder of Apple, revolutionized personal computing. Once Bill Gates retired from Microsoft, he moved into the sphere of philanthropy. In partnership with his wife, Melinda, they have transformed philanthropy by today's billionaire's and have made significant impact and change in global education and health.

Steve Jobs – was a business and technology genius. He envisioned a world that was not yet a reality. Imagine what it's like to see something that literally does not exist. Imagine painting that vision for early followers. Along with his peer, Bill Gates, as it related to the personal computer–they revolutionized the world.

Do you realize how momentous an achievement this was for Bill Gates and Steve Jobs? It's just as great as the discoveries of the ability to make and control fire, electricity or the telephone.

When a friend of mine was a little girl, her father was a computer systems analyst.

Laura describes growing up in a house with multiple floors. During those times in the 1970's and 1980's, her father had brought the home office to their house. She jokes that he was on the leading edge of being a remote worker.

It's not what you would imagine today.

Their basement had a raised floor with electrical cables snaking all over and air vents. Air conditioning kept the basement of their house cold. Mainframe computers that were as tall as an adult stood sentry. Tape machines and computer punch computers whirred day and night. Reams and reams of green and white paper printed dot matrix reports that would be unreadable to anyone who was not a computer geek.

Laura said that when she asked her father to teach her how to use a computer, he dropped a pile of manuals on the desk. Needless to say, she never learned. She was a generation removed from the real technological revolution growing up but today Laura works with a laptop, tablet and mobile device.

Had it not been for the inspired and visionary leadership of Bill Gates and Steve Jobs, none of what we see may have existed. Or if it did–maybe it would still be far off in the future. These leaders and others have created, changed and redefined whole industries and, quite literally, the world as it exists.

I have attended many board meetings in the nonprofit sector or have had conversations and I am still amazed when an executive director or CEO is asked about his or her vision and the individual stammers and is not able to articulate it well. I have seen it with large organizations and I have seen it with small ones.

Typically, these CEOs are able to explain well what their nonprofit is doing, but when you probe a little further and ask where the top person in the organization envisions the nonprofit in three or five years, I am met more often than I would like with awkward stammering.

This should never be the case.

Not today. Not ever.

Why is it that many nonprofit leaders believe they cannot look into the future without first discussing it with their board? They are too timid to share their vision without first having to discuss it with the board chair?

As I mentioned, in the past, I was leader of a nonprofit organization and I do understand the necessity to work closely with the board. However, often times, I see how this becomes a crutch that prevents the required creativity and forward movement necessary of today's successful organizations.

If you have worked or been involved in the nonprofit sector for a number of years, I am sure you can probably think of one or two examples of how a

CEO is relegated to a supporting cast member. The board becomes involved in the management of the agency somehow and soon the CEO is checking with the board about every minor decision he or she is making.

This is not leadership. This is simple dysfunction.

Excellent nonprofit leaders know they have to work with the board, but they also understand that they have a key role in educating the board as to their function and role. They understand that not only members of the senior management team and junior staff want to see leadership, but the board as well.

Very few individuals within an organization probably know the broad and minute details of the work done better than its CEO. At least they should. The best CEOs understand *all* aspects of his or her organization and this provides them with unparalleled information to truly set the vision and course for the path ahead.

The best nonprofit CEOs understand how the pieces fit and work together. He or she also understands the broader issues in society that relate to their mission. And with this knowledge, they should be able to articulate a bold and exciting vision. It does not matter if this is a large nonprofit or a small mom and pop organization.

This vision should excite not only staff, but the board as well and then supporters and the general public about the path forward. The best CEOs understand that they possess the ability to inspire people and call people to action. That is not the key role of the board, or of the staff. That is the primary role and function of the CEO.

He or she needs to have a thorough understanding of all of the issues inside and outside of the nonprofit as it relates to its mission and he or she needs to *not* be satisfied. This person then needs to be confident enough in his or her own abilities to risk articulating a path forward. Yes, of course, this person will get some push back and have grievances from people saying that it can't be done. But a well thought out vision and plan is a very precious thing.

If there is passion and drive to move in that direction, I can guarantee you that there will be people who will want to follow and support the effort. No great leader has ever had a path without obstacles. But, great leaders do not retreat at the first hint of adversity. Great leaders, in his or her own way, engage others and help them see a better world. This enables leaders to develop a group of followers, who provided the momentum for the push forward.

If you look at Steve Jobs and Bill Gates, they saw a vision for a world that did not yet exist. Yet, each in his business was able to communicate what the new world would mean. He created a story–something that humans have been doing since the beginning of time. And, with that story, each was able to develop followers who would take the risk with him to see to it that the world was made better in a new reality.

This included board members.

Sure, Steve Jobs was eventually ousted by the board at Apple only to be brought back into the circle after a number of years, but it was not before he played a pivotal role in revolutionizing computing. This could never have been done without the visionary's restlessness and a plan for the path forward.

Today's supporters are a disaffected lot. Particularly in the last twenty years, both young and old have seen incredible leaps forward. There was a time when something that happened on the other side of the world may not have made it to the evening's news because it would take days to get first-hand accounts, images and stories.

That is no longer the case. We live in a world that literally never sleeps. Something that happens on the other side of the planet can be broadcast to millions in an instant and in real time.

The nature of news itself has changed. Gone are the days when individuals sat in front of the television at the beginning of their evening home to catch up on the day's events. Increasingly gone are the network news channels. As the years pass, fewer and fewer people are relying on the network news anchor to rehash the news for them.

Cable and late night television have supplanted the news anchors. For immediacy Americans today will more likely turn to their computer or mobile device. They will search hashtags related to a global incident if it occurs and they will have a first hand account of events as they happen by citizen journalists and photographers. We each have the potential to be news reporters in the world today.

This means that leaders in the nonprofit sector have unprecedented ways to communicate with organizational champions, supporters and the general public. They need not rely on the traditional methods to reach out to people.

This easy communication provides an incredible opportunity to reward the visionary nonprofit risk takers who are not comfortable with the way things are, who want to change the status quo and want to be thought leaders.

I have written about this in a past article I wrote for my blog as it relates to the qualities of leadership for social entrepreneurs, but I believe these same qualities are also essential for nonprofit executives.

1. Temperament – successful nonprofit leaders need to be able to see

what others don't, which means they have to open the path. And, to do that, you need to have the right temperament. No matter what walk of life you find yourself in or place in the world, there will always be someone who will prefer to maintain the status quo or argue that what you think is possible is simply never going to happen. These naysayers will then provide a laundry list of reasons why something can't be done. Some who experience this push back will retreat and fall back into what they know. But, a true leader will use his or her charisma and powers of persuasion to mount a counter offensive. The leader will not seek to ram change through the organization, because he or she understands that in order to be successful, he or she must be able to obtain the buy-in of key stakeholders. So, while there may be moments of frustration, the leader will understand that fundamentally he or she needs to maintain inordinate amounts of optimism, a positive attitude and sense of humor. The old adage is very true: you catch more flies with honey than you do with vinegar. If people are continually being demeaned or lectured to, instead of brought on board as key individuals that will make a dream or vision a reality, they will follow grudgingly or do the bare minimums. Having a good temperament is the fundamental basis for everything else that will develop.

2. Creativity – Today, creativity is rewarded, stagnation is not. Imagine a world where Steve Jobs, Mark Zuckerberg, Bill and Melinda Gates simply said the change they were seeking could not be done. Perhaps in time, there would be someone else who would revolutionize computers, mobile, music, social media and philanthropy, but maybe the time would not have been now in the early 21st Century. These individuals, and so many others, have the courage to "think different." They understand that the same methods will produce the same results, which may be good in some instances, but certainly not all. So, they have each embarked on how to improve what we know of the world and that has involved creativity and innovation. When a leader is creative, he or she permits creativity to flow through the organization. Creativity is infectious and by modeling it, leaders give permission to their teams to think out of the box, or maybe even break the box and create something totally new if it will bring more impact and results.

3. Persistence – You can't quit. It is just not possible. I go back to Max

The Rise and Fail of Charities and What You Can Do To Be Ready
Wayne Elsey

Levchin, the co-founder of PayPal. He knew that there was a way to develop something that would revolutionize how people pay for things and send and receive money through the Internet in a way that was easier, faster and less expensive. Yet, the vision would not become the successful company until there were multiple failed attempts. Leaders will fail. This is part of life and it is part of business. However, leaders understand that they need to keep making their way forward, even after disappointment. And, they need to go further than the rest of their team. They not only have to suffer defeat, but they need to be the backbone for the team that relies on them to motivate and inspire past upsetting challenges and setbacks. This individual needs to stay the course.

4. Belief – Leaders need to have faith in their own vision and abilities. It is very easy for individuals to spot someone who does not believe in him or herself or in what they are saying. It's something someone can feel in his or her gut. Belief either exists or it doesn't. And, once a leader has belief in his or her vision, passion starts to bubble to the surface. That passion is something that permeates in the conversation the leader has with board members and staff. A genuine interest becomes evident as the leader asks the questions that staff and board members know are required to be asked in order to set the course. When there is belief, it permeates through everything that the leader does and says. You can't hide that.

Without those key ingredients, my belief is that a nonprofit leader will not be achieve results. All of the aforementioned qualities can be developed, if they are not naturally innate, but they mean the difference between success and failure.

If the leader does not have these characteristics, why should anyone choose to follow?

SEVEN
The Ingredients For Success in Today's World

Nonprofit Volunteer: I started volunteering to help kids. I loved the work, but I kept on getting asked for money. I was happy to give it, but somewhere along the line and the more I got involved, the less I understood where the money was going. I still volunteer helping the kids, but I am not giving more–no matter how many times they ask.

Success for today's nonprofits is one that has to break with a good portion of the past. The rapidly changing environment in which we all live and work demand it. Reward goes to those organizations, which innovate, are flexible, evolve, change and make a measurable impact.

If your organization has a database of donors who tend to skew toward the Boomers, you may be sitting confidently on your perch saying to yourself that none of what I wrote in this book relates to you.

Don't be mistaken. It does.

You are probably already experiencing a lack of trust capital with some donors and philanthropcapitalists who believe in bringing smart business practices into the nonprofit sector. You might be resisting, but you may be seeing the beginning trend of funders being less inclined to support your organization as they have done in the past.

Why? Donors can give their money elsewhere.

Take a look at your donor base and speak to your development and marketing professionals and ask them what keeps them awake at night.

I bet one of the major challenges is how to attract a new pipeline of donors and retain those who give once or sporadically. Perhaps your nonprofit looks more like your father or grandfather's charity rather than anything that would be successful going deep into the 21st Century.

How long can you rely on your current donor base without developing new strategies?

If you do not understand or agree with the premise that operating in today's business environment using staid and old methods is a problem, well, there is not much I can say that will convince you otherwise.

If, however, you see some of the following, if nothing else, take it from me– you need to rattle the cage a little:

- Your organization has experienced a persistent dip in funding because you are not attracting new prospects or significantly retaining current donors.
- Funders are asking you to provide information you were not asked to give five or even three years ago.
- You have Millennials on your staff continually knocking on your door providing you suggestions about how some systems can be done more efficiently and effectively with some low-cost technology.

So, if you believe, as I do, that you need to continually need to be reinventing and looking for how to do things better, where does an organization begin?

Well, as explained in the previous chapter, the first place to start is always with leadership.

If your board is stacked with people who would rather wear polyester than today's micro-breathing fabrics, you probably need to take a look at replacing a few members. If your executive is content simply maintaining the status quo of a bygone era, you probably need a change.

By the way, the following thoughts can be applied to both large and small nonprofits.

Mobile

If I were looking to create a new nonprofit or reinvigorate an existing one, after ensuring I had the best leadership and team on board for today's challenges, I would look at mobile.

Assuming you have a compelling story and all of the facts and images to support all of the wonderful impact that your organization is making, you want to be able to communicate your work for today's consumer and donor.

In a study done by Nielsen and Google[4], they found that 77 percent of mobile searches occur at home or in the office. So, people are always on their mobile devices: this despite the fact that they likely have a desktop computer or laptop at home or work.

More importantly, 3 out of 4 mobile searches trigger follow-up action. This can include a phone call, more research, and a purchase or word of mouth promotion to a peer.

Let's look at it another way so you can see the power of mobile. Currently, we have 7.1 billion people in the world. According to the United Nation's International Telecommunications Union, they estimated there would be nearly 7 billion mobile-cellular subscriptions globally[5]. As of my writing of this book, these numbers have not been updated.

In comparison, landlines were *never* this popular–and they never will be–they are a thing of the past. I can easily see a day when landlines are pretty much gone because people have cut the cord.

Today's tech leading giants are looking to ensure that every person on the face of the planet who is old enough to use a cell phone will have access to one. This is revolutionary. It means that banking, communications, work flow and commerce will inevitably change.

For those of us in developed countries who have access to multiple devices such as computers, tablets and cell phones, why do so many searches today occur on mobile devices?

Well, think about it.

More than likely, you have your tablet or cell phone with you at all times, day or night. Today's mobile phones are like jewelry or a watch. It is always on the person or within very quick reach. This is why we are now seeing the evolution of wearable technology. Someday, you may find donors making a gift after doing a search for information on your nonprofit on their smart watch.

The same Nielsen and Google study found that 81 percent of mobile searches were driven by speed and convenience. I am guilty of it and I am sure you are too. Even if a computer is nearby, I may quickly grab my cell phone to do a quick search.

4   "Mobile Search Moments" Study, Think With Google, March 2013, https://www.thinkwith-google.com/research-studies/creating-moments-that-matter.html

5   "Statistics_Page_All_Charts_2014," Excel File Download, http://www.itu.int/en/ITU-D/Statistics/Pages/stat/default.aspx

Nonprofits need to ensure that their websites, which is the *first* place a prospective donor or someone looking for information on your organization will go, are optimized for mobile. This is an absolute must in today's world. With technology becoming very competitive in terms of price point, there is simply no excuse for even the smallest nonprofit to not be completely mobile ready.

Content Marketing

The next thing I would take a look at is high quality content marketing. Here's the deal, some "old school" ideas and principles never change because they stand the test of time.

Humans will always seek information. From the earliest of times when cave people were writing stories on walls to social media, stories can help drive a movement or protest. Humans will always want to know, learn and gain understanding through information and stories.

That being said, the people who are living today have been bombarded with advertising and marketing and they are not interested in another "sales" approach about how your company, business or nonprofit can change their lives.

They immediately tune out and with the ease of technology they can skip through obvious and unnecessary promotion or avoid them all together. Today's marketing professionals have had to seek new and innovative ways to reach their target audience. Nonprofits need to follow suit.

Therefore, today's leading businesses, social enterprises and nonprofits understand that content is still king. But in order to truly engage with their audience, they need to provide information donors and other stakeholders care to know. Content marketing is much more customer, or in the case of nonprofits, donor focused.

High quality content that your donors care to read is what you should be in the business of curating and producing. Individuals and funders who want to build a relationship with you want to understand how the issues you address impact the world in which we live.

This means that you need to continually be providing information that helps educate and inform them. This, in turn, engages them and ultimately will produce increased donations to your organization.

Writing a newsletter once a month is simply not going to cut it.

First of all, good luck on having many people read your newsletter in between the hundreds of emails that any one individual receives on any given day. In order for your organization not to be lost in the shuffle, you need to be able to provide engaging content *and* it has to be delivered to your constituents in ***multiple*** ways.

This means in order for your message to get through that your donors need to be seeing electronic newsletters, video, images, blogs, articles, books or guides being written by your nonprofit. The organization has to position itself as a thought leader as it relates to the mission. All of this helps to develop and enrich the relationship your organization will have with its donors.

And, today's content marketing world is well suited to a mobile world where people are incessantly obtaining information on news apps, through video, on social media and by doing Internet searches. Therefore, as a reminder, when you are putting out all of your brilliant content, make sure it is accessible easily from a mobile device. It can very well be the difference between getting your next donation or not.

There is a warning, however. Once you set forth on a strategic content marketing effort, you may find someone on your team who wants to rely only on automation. Automation is great, but it is not the end all and be all. And, if you rely solely on automation to curate content, you will be disappointed when you review and analyze your ROI.

You simply can't "set it and forget it." You need to constantly be looking at what's happening in your world and getting that information out to your followers. You need to be able to provide a mix of news specific to your organization and broader stories that are related to the work you do. This helps to inform them and keep them up to date on relevant topics.

Marketing is something that is sometimes misunderstood by executives in the nonprofit sector. It seems they can have a better handle on programs and fundraising, because you can see more easily report on all of the quantitative data. However, I have heard professional marketing officers in the nonprofit sector consistently try to determine ways to justify their positions.

This should never be the case.

Nonprofit executives need to understand that marketing officers represent an essential aspect of the team, just as important as the program or fundraising officers.

Nonprofit CEOs sometime look at the marketing budget and use it as one of the first areas to cut during lean times. Other times, nonprofit executives look at their marketing dollars as needing to be solely dedicated to maintaining communication with existing funders and obtaining new donors.

Because nonprofit organizations have multiple stakeholders, including the general tax paying public, government, the media, funders, other nonprofits, etc., marketing should be a leading and strategic part of the whole operation.

Successful marketing officers are able to help develop and clarify an organization's brand and positioning in the sector. And, they are able to develop key messaging so there is consistency in communication across all platforms for all stakeholders.

Marketing officers help to raise awareness of not only the brand, but about the cause. They help develop and curate information that all of your stakeholders want to see in your content marketing.

In addition, they help in organizational advocacy efforts and promotion of events and program initiatives. Marketing should be something that threads through every aspect of your organization.

So, the next time you are viewing marketing narrowly as only related to fundraising or as so un-necessary that it can successfully operate after you take a budget hatchet to it instead of a scalpel, take a moment and think again. Marketing is just as important as your programmatic and fundraising teams.

And, that leads me to the next thing I would look at if I were seeking to establish a new nonprofit or reignite the efforts of one that has grown old and tired.

Team Work

There is no success that I have professionally achieved or that of any of the companies and organizations I have worked for or built without the combined efforts of the team I have worked with at any given time.

The fact of the matter is no nonprofit board or executive is an island. A solid, passionate, driven and motivated team of professionals is essential to success.

If you surf the Internet for even a little bit, you will find countless articles about the tensions that exist between Millennials and Boomers in the work place. Some of it may be accurate.

It's true that generations that come before always have a little issue when they suddenly see they are being told that there is a better way to do something by someone who may be more than half their age. But, I also think a lot of what is stated as fact is simple hyperbole.

We live in a world where so many things can be done with the use of technology. And each year we read how computers and robots will eventually replace human workers, I don't think that will wholly be true–at least not in our lifetimes.

So, as far as I am concerned, workers are an essential part of a successful nonprofit or for-profit enterprise.

If you were to come into my office today, you would see diversity and that is something that I am very proud of ensuring. Among other things, you would see men and women of differing generations, races and backgrounds working together to achieve success across all of our businesses.

In addition, you would discover that I have individuals who work with me remotely in other parts of the country and the world. That is the benefit of technology. I can be working based on east coast time, but each working day, I have other people in other time zones working to help me ensure the success of our businesses. We are "on" 24 hours a day.

My businesses are working around the clock and leveraging the best resources, no matter where they are located, to produce high quality results.

So, the nature of how we work together and collaborate has certainly changed in the 21st Century.

I have written in the past about the challenges in pay that exist in the nonprofit sector. This exists at the CEO level, but it also very much exists at the more junior levels. When I have stated this, I have had people tell me that salaries must be kept "very low" so that most of the money raised can go to programs.

I am not going to debate the merits or lack thereof of that position in this particular book; however, what I am going to acknowledge is that the vast majority of nonprofits operate with budgets of less than $1 million.

If you are a nonprofit board member or executive reading this book, chances are that you have limited resources. However, that is not an excuse not to be able to be good to your team. Providing the right mix of incentives and rewards will only enhance your work environment and organizational success.

Putting the topic of compensation to the side, there are definite strategies you can use to help retain the best workers.

Today's employees need to be continually learning. In fact, everyone has to be continually educating him or herself and keeping their skills sharp. This is particularly true around technology and how it can be incorporated into respective team roles. However, with technology, new best practices around work functions begin to develop. Therefore, today's worker needs to be on a lifetime path for knowledge.

Young Millennials intrinsically know this. They grew up in a world where they saw constant change and the signal to them was that the world was full of change.

Other generations came of age and were adults during times that were less revolutionary in terms of the pace and advancement of science, technology and business processes. Therefore, those individuals have had to adapt and understand that nothing remains the same. If they want to remain competitive, they need to reinvent themselves. They also need to develop new ways of thinking so they too get on the track for continual learning and adaptation, especially as it relates to technology.

Thus, professional development is an element that not only young professionals, but also more senior workers would appreciate.

Today's worker knows, as fact, that he or she must always be developing their skills. Therefore, it behooves nonprofits to invest in developing and growing the skills for their work teams. Courses, seminars, conferences related to someone's role within an organization are beneficial and rewarding to the team members who participate.

It also allows the nonprofit to obtain intellectual knowledge that can be executed by that person to enhance processes and procedures in accomplishing someone's job.

We all know that work and home life are no longer mutually exclusive. The two have melded. Therefore, good leaders need to provide their work teams flexibility. For some nonprofits, this may mean opportunities to work from home. For other organizations it may mean flexible work schedules so workers are able to tend to issues that might come up with their children, health or even their aging parents.

Flexibility should not be feared because the vast majority of workers will not abuse it. In fact, they will appreciate it. Further, we know that high quality work can be produced and submitted, if say for instance, a parent has to stay home with a sick child. More than likely the parent would be less productive if he or she were forced to be in the office because the parent's mind would be elsewhere.

Money is a motivator. I don't believe it should be the only motivator, but it is a good motivator nonetheless. For organizations that may not have the financial budget to compensate their workers with more competitive salaries, a retention strategy would be to offer a more generous benefits package.

In addition, bonuses are very good motivators. Nonprofits can create individual and team competitions on projects and reward excellence and success for exceeding goals with monetary bonuses. More than likely, this would place *less* of a strain on tight nonprofit budgets, but it would be something that workers would appreciate.

As it relates to team, I am also a believer in mentorship. I think more seasoned workers have enormous value and they likely retain high degrees of institutional knowledge. Sometimes, I have seen nonprofit organizations dismiss more senior employees simply because they think that person is an "old horse." But, they have failed to invest in any professional development or challenge that individual to adapt and evolve.

A perfect opportunity exists, in some of the instances I have seen, where mutual mentorship would be the perfect antidote to the inexperience of a young worker and, perhaps, the lack of a high degree of technological sophistication of a more senior employee.

There are wonderful opportunities for fundraisers, for example, who understand how to close a gift of $100,000 to learn how to effectively use YouTube, Facebook or Twitter for donations.

Nonprofit CEOs should foster an environment where it is all right *not* to know something. No one should feel insecure about saying they don't know something.

In fact, you want to know when there is a knowledge deficit. The reality is no one can possibly know everything. But the caveat should be that anything that is not known would be earnestly explored and learned.

Investment

I would put away the tin cup. Let's stop talking all the time about charity, which only addresses the immediate symptoms of a social challenge. Let's also have substantial conversations about addressing the root causes of a poor education system, for example, and also make the connection to poverty. Or let's talk about poverty, and address the lack of work opportunity.

Let's talk about philanthropy.

And, in those discussions, let's talk about investment. Nonprofits are businesses. Executives and boards need to *always* keep this in mind. Today's donors and leading philanthrocapitalists understand that in order to truly make things happen, we need to invest. Look at the donations made by funders as an investment in your nonprofit to make an impact.

I have heard forward-thinking nonprofit leaders say in the past that they are in the business of being taken out of business because they have solved and beaten the societal challenge of their mission.

That's smart thinking.

Nonprofits should want to get to that point where they discovered *the* solution, implemented it, brought it to scale or replicated it, demonstrated results and then closed their doors.

I am not the only one who believes that a great error of the nonprofit sector, at least in the United States, was assuming their "nonprofit" tax designation was some sort of business model.

I have had executives who have shared with me the incredible amount of time they had to spend educating board members on how it is acceptable for a nonprofit to actually have a **surplus** in its budget so long as it gets reinvested in the organization.

Still, there has been a failure by nonprofit executives, donors, funders and even the general public, which created a myth that nonprofits have an obligation to solve the world's problems on a shoestring budget.

Funders today are demanding metrics, accountability, transparency and impact. By default, this means that nonprofit organizations **must** make an investment into their infrastructure in order to be able to meet all of those demands. It can't be done with Band-Aids.

Individual and institutional donors need to become comfortable with the fact that in order to truly have a sense of how a nonprofit is performing in every area of its business operation, it requires money. Zero costs for operation is simply not credible or believable.

Additionally, nonprofit boards and executives need to absorb the fact that **they are a business** that serves society. They also need to believe they are worthy of investment dollars for better skilled workers, professional development, program development, technology and infrastructure.

Without this change in mindset from those within and outside of the nonprofit sector, there will simply be more opportunity for corporations and social enterprises with investment money to fill the space.

EIGHT
Philanthropy's Time Has Arrived

Philanthropcapitalist: I am always looking to get to the root of the problem. I have the money to give millions if I wanted to, but I don't. I have charities come to me every day. But, I probably support only 5 percent. I'm not looking for the same sorry story of need. Tell me how you are changing it. Set the vision.

Throughout history, leading philanthropists have wanted to move away from charity and focus at the root of societal problems and practice philanthropy. During his time, Andrew Carnegie propagated this thinking, as did John D. Rockefeller.

I believe that with today's resources, the vision of these philanthropic leaders of yesterday and the philanthropcapitalists of today, making the shift from focusing on charity to philanthropy is attainable.

During the course of writing this book, I have wanted to convey the message of change. Even if you don't think change is happening, and oftentimes it does not seem so, it is.

The donors of today are very sophisticated. It doesn't matter who they are. You need to assume that even a college student has done his or her homework on your organization before you see them volunteer or provide you with a donation.

The information superhighway that is the Internet has placed in front of people vast troves of information at unprecedented levels. There really is no way that people won't know about you, or shouldn't know about you. That's the whole point in today's world.

Leading nonprofits, large and small, want to seek a position that has them prominently placed as thought leaders in an organization that is highly transparent and accountable to its donors and the public. Organizations that do not foster and maintain a high level of trust capital, by demonstrating that they can operate in this brave new world are ultimately doomed to fail.

Nonprofits are indeed a business, as much as some in the industry might grumble. And, as businesses, which happen to support society, they must begin to adhere more and more to solid business principles, especially as it relates to money.

Governments are cutting back the funding and support that they provided post-war and especially since the beginning of the Great Recession. A confluence of events, including great advances in technology, information sharing and science have conspired to put nonprofits in a position to respond to a major paradigm shift that is affecting their marketing, programs, operational and fundraising efforts.

All of this is working to force nonprofits to be more flexible, innovative, forward thinking, technologically adept, socially and publicly aware. This means that the old tin cup and timid nonprofit leadership will not work any longer.

Why should any donor give even a $1 to any organization that year after year stays the same, or worse, contracts? Organizations are competing with social enterprises and big business, and that alone is forcing change.

Nonprofit board members and executives need to forget the "not-for-profit" part, with the exception of when it is doing its legal and accounting reporting. Organizations must move to look at themselves as businesses that want to grow and thrive. Their "profit" is measured by the social capital it provides in the fulfillment of its mission.

Donors and nonprofits need to understand and internalize that these organizations, in fact, do need to have investment. Money is absolutely necessary for success. Donors and nonprofits have to have ongoing conversations about what is needed to succeed as businesses that support the social sector.

We have to move away from the concept of constant and unending charity. Yes, we need to figure out effective ways to certainly address immediate needs. However, we also need to target the deeper issues that cause poverty, create situations where education is lacking, destroy the environment or foster inequality.

The Rise and Fail of Charities and What You Can Do To Be Ready
Wayne Elsey

We have to talk philanthropically.

Yes, we have to support people, for example, who find themselves enduring tough times and help them out. We need to be charitable, but our efforts as a whole should be much more philanthropic.

In the work I do, I always believe in teaching someone to fish rather than simply giving someone a fish, which will only feed the individual for a day. I believe wholeheartedly in philanthropy.

When I saw the need of poor families in developing nations to have shoes, which are necessary for individuals to attend school or obtain a job, I believed in developing a way to get shoes to them.

But, I wanted to go deeper.

Why did people not have shoes? They were too poor to be able to afford them.

Why were they too poor? Families lacked opportunity to well-paying jobs.

And, so I developed a program to support micro-enterprise in developing countries. I took a philanthropic view at the challenge of poverty.

Nonprofits should be about going from serving one classroom to serving many; from building one wired library to building many; from saving one whale to saving many; or from curing one aspect of a disease to curing the disease itself.

Successful organizations understand that in order to make an impact it needs to be deep, but often it also needs to be broad and systemic.

That is why in the new century you have seen nonprofits and social enterprises start off from nothing to become multi-million dollar organizations. These organizations understand that they need to grow to scale and they are looking to focus on the whole of an issue, not simply one piece of it.

Yes, not every school needs to be like a KIPP Academy school, for example, which was founded in Texas and now has schools in other parts of the nation.

Yes, not every hospital needs to grow into a medical center.

But, there is certainly room for *countless* other nonprofits to grow and replicate their programs beyond their local community.

Words are nice, but they need to be followed by action. Saying that you want to lead a 21st Century nonprofit is all well and good, but it has to be followed with concrete actions that communicate to those around you, including funders, that you understand what that means.

Trust capital is not only important. It is crucially important. And nonprofit organizations that are not building it are failing.

Donors and the public want to see success in using today's methods and principles, which oftentimes do have a basis in the past, but are adapted to the current environment.

Nonprofits need to take a leading role in the conversation, or as I have stated, the conversations will happen without them at the table.

This means that nonprofit executives need to become very well schooled and educated on what it means to be a leader in today's organizations. Board members as well have a responsibility to educate themselves around the best practices that are being adapted from business and brought into the nonprofit sector.

I have worked in both the for-profit and the non-profit industries. Some nonprofit executives would argue with me and say that the industry needs to be careful and stay pure to its nonprofit roots.

Frankly, I think they're wrong.

No one is saying that nonprofits need to be for-profit ventures. We are not looking at a world where nonprofits will become accountable to shareholder profits. And, yes, there is a world that exists right now where nonprofits are indeed accountable to tax payers, donors, the general public and society itself. This means nonprofits have more oversight and regulation.

But, we need to take the training wheels off the nonprofit sector and force the industry to become much more competitive. Business principles around marketing, investment and research and development do, in fact, need to be incorporated more into the nonprofit sector.

We know that many nonprofit program executives are experts at what they do. They live and breathe the social issues they are looking to address.

Tell me, what program officer would not want to see more investment into his or her work?

What program officer would not want to see the organization expand and help affect the lives of countless more?

I don't think I have ever met a program officer who wants less investment and fewer resources.

If some general donors, major donors and billionaire philanthropists are saying that they want to see excellence in programs and in impact, don't you think this means that we need to have a change in the conversation within the industry?

Don't you think this means we need to stop talking only about charity and start talking about philanthropy as well? Don't you think it means supporting nonprofit missions with all of today's resources brought to bear? We have *enor-*

mous resources of money, technology and intellect.

I think, at least in the United States, we would be in a better position to see a smaller number of nonprofits serving larger numbers than millions serving few. Again, there is room for small charities, but there is a lot of redundancy.

Last week I received a call from a fundraiser. My friend was going on about how yet another nonprofit was being established to help support education. Denise has many years in the business and she's earned the right to tell it like is. So, she asked the new nonprofit how it is different than the countless nonprofits doing the same thing?

She told me she knew very quickly—within seconds—that she did not want to work with them, but she also was hoping they would see how very difficult it is to be truly excellent.

Denise has been in so many of these conversations and they all seem to turn out the same. After listening and conversing with them for a while, she saw yet another nonprofit organization being founded. It will probably serve a handful of children, at best.

They ignored questions of vision and even some practical advice she was telling them based on her years in the business. The advice was around some low cost ways to use technology to fundraise and how to structure a board that helps support fundraising.

And here we go again, she thought, another nonprofit trying to take up valuable resources.

She confided in me that she hoped they would fail quickly and spectacularly. The leadership had no idea how to lead and it was just going to be an exercise in frustration. They failed to see how to do even the most basic things to position themselves ahead. More importantly, they didn't want to see. They believed it they build it, people will want to give to it.

They were myopic in only seeing they wanted to help kids, but were not open to listening to an expert's advice and counsel on how to get there. The story was not compelling enough. Everyone wants to help kids! How is your story different? What are you going to do better than the other organization down the block that is doing the same thing? Or, how do you intend to compete with the larger organizations that operate in the same space?

I remember Denise's chuckle when she said, "Oh, Wayne, it's a case of 'not your father's charity again.'" It's old school thinking in a brave new world. It's just talking charity, when leaders are looking at philanthropy.

We are at the beginning of a whole new conversation on philanthropy. Or, you can say that we are ending the decades long conversation we have been having about charity.

Nonprofits have served a great place in the social society of the United States and they **still** have a role to play going forward.

However, the only ones that will continue to rise successfully are those that have strong nonprofit leaders. These leaders need to communicate, inform and educate the public and donors about the resources they need. These leaders need to have a big vision, which is threaded through with bold and innovative ideas.

Donors don't want to "make a difference." They want to "make it happen." They want to end educational inequality, poverty, disease and the strain on the environment. And, today, nonprofits are not the only kid on the block. Supporters will naturally gravitate to the organizations, for-profits or nonprofits that are leading the way and demonstrating results.

Anything less than being **the** best is simple complacency. There is no more room for "almost."